SCHELLING'S TREATISE ON
"THE DEITIES OF SAMOTHRACE"

AMERICAN ACADEMY OF RELIGION
STUDIES IN RELIGION

edited by
Stephen Crites

Number 12

SCHELLING'S TREATISE ON "THE DEITIES OF SAMOTHRACE"
A Translation and An Interpretation
by
Robert F. Brown

SCHOLARS PRESS
Missoula, Montana

SCHELLING'S TREATISE ON "THE DEITIES OF SAMOTHRACE"
A Translation and An Interpretation

by
Robert F. Brown

Published by
SCHOLARS PRESS
for
The American Academy of Religion

Distributed by

SCHOLARS PRESS
University of Montana
Missoula, Montana 59812

SCHELLING'S TREATISE ON "THE DEITIES OF SAMOTHRACE"
by
Robert F. Brown

Library of Congress Cataloging in Publication Data

Brown, Robert F.   1941-
   Schelling's Treatise on "The deities of Samothrace."

   (Studies in religion ; no. 12)
   Bibliography: p.
   1. Schelling, Friedrich Wilhelm Joseph von, 1775-
1854. Ueber die Gottheiten von Samothrace. 2. Myth-
ology, Greek. 3. Samothrace—Religion. I. Schelling,
Friedrich Wilhelm Joseph von, 1775-1854. Ueber die
Gottheiten von Samothrace. English. 1976. II. Title.
III. Series: American Academy of Religion. AAR studies
in religion ; no. 12.
BL793.S3S332   292'.2'11   76-42239
ISBN 0-89130-087-2

ω

Printed in the United States of America

Printing Department
University of Montana
Missoula, Montana 59812

CONTENTS

PREFACE

Access to the actual beliefs of ancient peoples does not come easily to modern investigators. In and behind the myths, inscriptions, artifacts, and traveller's accounts lies a world (or perhaps multiple worlds) of meanings only partially glimpsed through the traces left to the historian. In the early nineteenth century many persons engaged in scholarship or in the creative arts shared in common a fascination with the aesthetic and symbolic features of ancient mythologies, especially that of the Greeks. The rejuvenation of classical studies in the late eighteenth century led directly to the unbounded enthusiasm for ancient Greece among the Romantics at the outset of the nineteenth century. Although they were strongly influenced by the intellectual tradition of confessional Christianity, some German philosophers and theologians of the time nevertheless became intrigued with the prospect of transcending a narrowly Christian perspective (more particularly, that of Lutheran Protestantism). Bold moves in this direction were encouraged by the convergence of liberalizing and rationalizing tendencies in theology, by the renewed respect and admiration for the pre-Christian world of ancient Greece, and also by the beginnings of access to reliable knowledge of other Asian religions heretofore known dimly or not at all. Among the giants of this enterprise in Germany were Schleiermacher on the theological side, and Hegel and Schelling on the philosophical side. This study is a translation and an interpretation of the treatise, *The Deities of Samothrace,* by F. W. J. Schelling (1775 - 1854), who made in it a sympathetic interpretation of an instance of ancient Greek mythology and religious cult, and thereby integrated his understanding of its inner meaning into his own philosophical system. The treatise is of interest both as a specific example of the interpretation of Greek mythology and mystery religion by a leader of Romanticism and of German Idealism, and also as a key transitional work in Schelling's own long and varied philosophical career. The latter theme will receive greater emphasis here, for the primary purpose of this study is to contribute to our understanding of Schelling's later philosophy.

I wish to acknowledge the contributions of other scholars to the completion of this project. A session of the Nineteenth Century Theology Group of the American Academy of Religion, devoted to "Myth and Symbol, 1800 - 1848: The Role of Schelling," provided the original stimulus for making the translation and a forum for discussing my interpretation of the text. Stephen D. Crites of Wesleyan University, the editor of this monograph series, meticulously compared the translation with the original and thereby helped me to correct a few errors and to avoid a number of infelicities of style. He also suggested recasting the format of the introductory and interpretive materials in my original paper into a more suitable arrangement for monograph presentation. Gerald R. Culley of the Department of Languages and Literature of the University of Delaware gave assistance in transliteration and in the translation of a letter from Latin, as well as advice on other matters. Alfred R. Wedel and James C. Davidheiser, also of the same Department, helped me with several difficulties in translating Schelling's German. Robert E. A. Palmer of the Department of Classical Studies, the University of Pennsylvania, made several suggestions which improved the translation and the handling of the classical sources. Of course any remaining errors of translation or interpretation are my own responsibility.

ROBERT F. BROWN
Newark, Delaware
September, 1975

Part One

Translator's Introduction

1. Context in Schelling's Authorship

The Deities of Samothrace[1] is an address which Schelling presented on October 12, 1815 in the public session of the Bavarian Academy of Sciences, held in honor of the nameday of its patron, King Maximilian IV Joseph of Bavaria (reigned 1806 - 1825). Schelling had been appointed the first Director of the new Academy of the Arts division at its formation in 1806. Therefore it was highly appropriate for him to be invited to speak on this occasion and for him to choose a topic of major importance in the current development of his own thought. Although he promptly published his address, it unfortunately received little notice from his contemporaries and no sustained attention has been given to it in subsequent Schelling scholarship. Probably the reason his contemporaries disregarded it was that Schelling had already entered a period of eclipse so far as the public was concerned, an eclipse which was to persist (except for a brief interruption in 1834 when he launched an attack on Hegel's philosophy) until 1841 when, with much fanfare, he resumed lecturing at Berlin.

Schelling had published a great many essays during the decade of his twenties (1795 - 1804), a number of them being philosophical work of high quality. Throughout this period he enjoyed vast popular acclaim and shared jointly with Fichte the honor of being the acknowledged successor to Kant. His well-known displacement from the public eye after 1804 was not due solely to the publication of Hegel's *Phenomenology of Spirit* (1807), which certainly elevated its author to the position of leadership of the post-Kantian idealists. It was also the result of events in Schelling's personal life, of a severely reduced rate of writing and publication, and most especially a consequence of the fact that his own thought was in ferment. Somewhere in the middle of this first decade of the nineteenth century Schelling began to read seriously the works of Jacob Boehme (1575 - 1624). The consequence was a dramatic shift in his thought, the first concrete evidence of which was the publication of the essay *Of Human Freedom* in 1809.[2]

1

In his new phase Schelling became preoccupied with the problems of free will and of the relation of being to non-being. The manuscripts from the years 1809 - 1815 show him working out the details of a voluntaristic ontology which comprises a unique vision of the natures of both God and the world.[3] The essay *Of Human Freedom* developed into an attempt to construct an adequate theodicy, based on a speculative view of the divine nature derived from Boehme. In it Schelling presented for the first time his new doctrine of a bipolar God who contains an element of dialectical non-being within his own nature. It was regrettable that his exploratory essay of 1809 left a number of corollary issues unexamined, because the major essays immediately following which elaborated the details of the new system were never published in his lifetime.

In 1810 Schelling gave a series of private lectures at Stuttgart to a small group of friends at the home of E. F. Georgii.[4] In this text we find further refinements of his conception of God and a thorough outline of the structures of human and sub-human nature which fills out the new ontology. He next composed two controversial essays in which he responded formally to his critics, one response being extremely hostile and polemical (to F. H. Jacobi, 1811)[5] and the other cordial and constructive (to K. A. Eschenmayer, 1812).[6] In both responses Schelling found himself in the disadvantageous posture of defending ideas stated in *Of Human Freedom* without being able to invoke the refined version of his position in the *Stuttgart Lectures,* which was unpublished and therefore unknown to all but the original auditors.

After the *Stuttgart Lectures,* Schelling set to work on the third and final major essay in the explication of his new speculative doctrine of God, *The Ages of the World* (1811 - 1815).[7] In *Ages* he spelled out in great detail a portrait of a bipolar God in whom will and freedom prevail over being and necessity, a God who freely constructs his own eternal nature and then, again freely, wills to create a world comprised of the same structural principles and powers which constitute the divine being itself. In carrying out the plan of *Ages,* which remains an unfinished work, Schelling saw the need to validate his merely speculative concept of God by seeking confirmation of it in the documented evidence of mythology and religious practice in human history. This was a logical step to take because his speculative position is pervaded with the systematic conviction that the structures of God and of his creation parallel one another, and that God uses his creation, especially the development of human consciousness throughout history, as the means of his self-revelation. Therefore one should be able to come to the same concept of God as that reached in his metaphysical speculation, by proceeding from the other direction, from an understanding of the world. This quest eventually led Schelling on to the massive study of mythology and revelation which occupied the greater part of his energies in the remaining decades of his long career. (He lectured on these topics earlier than 1841, but all the lecture manuscripts in the collected works date from 1841 - 1852.) Although the concluding parts of

Ages contain fragmentary "evidence" in confirmation of his speculation, largely drawn from the Old Testament, the work as a whole remains under the spell of purely metaphysical reflection. The project of the system's historical validation actually began in a modest way with *The Deities of Samothrace,* which Schelling subtitled a "supplement" to *Ages.* In it he aspired to conjure up, through historical-philological study of ancient texts, the authentic residue of the original religion of the human race which he fully expected would be consonant with his own speculative philosophical theology.

Because *Ages* remained unpublished, Schelling's contemporaries had no access to the detailed philosophical theology which lay immediately behind his interpretation of the Samothracian system. Therefore it is not surprising that the work was little noted or understood at the time. It is somewhat more surprising that later scholarship which is well acquainted with *Ages* has paid so little attention to *The Deities of Samothrace,* a transitional work coming at one of the key junctures in Schelling's career. This treatise is an instructive example of how Schelling interrelated the metaphysical (speculative) and the empirical (historical) components in his subsequent efforts to comprehend the structure and implicit content of all human religious experience and mythological expression.[8] Through this translation and interpretation I hope to make *The Deities of Samothrace* accessible and thus more widely known and appreciated among students of German Idealism and of the history of religions and the philosophy of mythology as these disciplines developed in the early nineteenth century.

In the remainder of this Translator's Introduction I will present a variety of background information which I hope will be useful to one reading the text for the first time. The systematic analysis of Schelling's interpretation of the Samothracian gods is reserved for Part Three. It shows in detail how Schelling rendered the symbolism of the Samothracian gods so that it corresponds to his own recently-modified ontology, and it also discusses the momentum which *The Deities of Samothrace* gave to the much more ambitious historical investigations of mythology and revelation in the later works. The focus of this study is on what Schelling makes of the Samothracian system in the context of his own thought and age, and not on a critique of his views in light of subsequent archaeological discoveries and scholarship on Greek antiquities.[9] To the classical scholar of today Schelling's essay may seem an outdated curiosity. But my concern is to use it to enlarge our understanding of Schelling as a nineteenth century philosopher of religion and comparative mythologist.

2. Why Samothrace?

Schelling was highly trained in classical studies, and may well have surpassed his great contemporaries Hegel and Schleiermacher in the breadth of his knowledge of ancient languages and literatures. Besides the massive lectures on mythology, his collected works contain a number of short articles, lectures and reviews concerning historical and philological topics from the ancient world. Why did Schelling specifically choose to study the religion of Samothrace, and why do so at just this point in his career? The text itself discloses both general and special reasons for his choice.

In a time when more sophisticated techniques of historical research were developing, aided by the budding science of archaeology, any major site of antiquity could be singled out as a worthy object of study. Schelling calls attention to the relative neglect of Samothrace in his day particularly because he regards the mystery cult surrounding the Samothracian deities as the oldest, and perhaps the noblest, of ancient Greece.[10] But his special interest derives from what he expects to find there, namely,

> . . . monuments of the most ancient belief, even more important than the former (i. e. works of art) for the entire history of our species. (349)

The obscurity surrounding the names and significance of these gods and goddesses must be dispelled, for Schelling believes that the religion of Samothrace contains the key to an original system of belief antedating and underlying the varied mythologies and revelations of human history. His footnote 90 (to p. 362) states:

> . . . the text . . . only sets forth as a possibility, the existence of such a primordial system older than all written documents, which is the common source of all religious doctrines and representations. . . .

Therefore the meanings to be unearthed from the records of the Samothracian cult should disclose original and fundamental structures of human mythological and religious consciousness. It is nothing less than this that Schelling is after, and Samothrace is the place where he thinks it best may be found.

3. Some Methodological Points.

Although Schelling generally is aware of the issues at stake in choosing an approach to a difficult subject, explicit methodological statements are not very numerous in this essay. Early in the work he expresses reservations about assuming that deities with similar names necessarily stand for comparable concepts, and offers cautionary words about hasty conclusions on the relation of public to secret doctrines (349). His discussion of method focuses in the main on historical and philological procedures, whereas the way in which he himself applies speculative philosophical categories to the historical data remains unexamined. Commentary on this latter and most important issue is reserved for Part Three, in the explanation of his ontological categories in their application to Samothrace. Here I mention only those historical aspects of method to which Schelling himself refers.

Schelling's research and conclusions are based on literary sources from ancient times, and his interpretation of them is guided to some extent by the writings of later classical scholars. It does not appear that he is relying on any recent archaeological work, or in fact on any artifacts other than some monuments and tombstone inscriptions (347, 356). As an historian dealing principally with texts his attention concentrates on the names of the deities and what can be discovered from them by the science of philology. Evidently in his day the derivation of concepts from linguistic structures was under something of a cloud, at least in its application to religion and mythology. Nevertheless he is confident that it can be practiced in a reputable and disciplined way if one follows definite rules (351).

Schelling states three concrete guidelines for his philological labors. The first is that because Phoenician and Hebrew are cognate languages, etymologies in one language are applicable to the other as well. This emphasis is correlative with his conclusion that the Cabiri cult was brought to Samothrace by Phoenician sailors, and with his desire (already seen in *Ages*) to find in the Old Testament traces of the "original system of belief." The second guideline is that because proper names in Oriental languages are meaningful words the names can and do express concepts. Finally, he insists that the meanings derived from the names of the deities must be specific ones; abstract generalities applicable to any and every deity will not suffice.

Because Schelling regards this last point as quite important, he presents it emphatically in his note 29 (to p. 351). To remove the stigma which some in his day apparently attached to such interpretations, in a time when

> . . . a new frenzy of linguistic derivations struggled to produce everything from everything, and mixed all things together in a crazy manner even in the old stories of the gods, . . .

one must insist on precision and on attention to context. Usually a deity is represented as possessing a considerable range of attributes. Schelling derides the practice of those who rest content with finding some one general meaning of the deity's name which has some plausible connection with one of its attributes. To do so is uninformative, and fails to capture the precision with which (so he declares) ancient peoples conceptualized their gods. Instead, interpretation must be systematic.

> Therefore above all else it is necessary for the researcher to know the basic concept of a deity, the root as it were of all its attributes. . . . But these fundamental concepts are only determined through the position which each deity occupies in the general system of the gods. (Note 29 to p. 351)

In philological terms, one must uncover the contextual meaning of the name in its ancient use. In addition to his explicitly stated rules (351, also note 29 to p. 351) one also cannot help being conscious of the unmentioned rule which Schelling consistently employs: the interpretation of ancient deities and their mutual relations must be philosophically systematic. For Schelling the "correct" etymologies are those which clear the way for assigning the deity in question a meaning and role in a pantheon having a systematic metaphysical structure.

One other methodological point has to do with the common practice among the German Idealists of giving to the biblical religions a sympathetic interpretation, but not one controlled by confessional theological methods. In *Ages* Schelling did this with Old Testament materials. Here in the present text he remarks:

> The Hebrew language and writings, foremost the Old Testament, in which the roots
> of doctrine and the language itself of all ancient religious systems are clearly
> recognizable down to details, lie unstudied. (note 113 to p. 367)

What a scandal to tell biblical scholars that the texts remain unstudied! But obviously Schelling means unstudied from any other standpoint than that of the quest for confirmation of Jewish or Christian orthodoxies. In note 113 he declares that the "purely historical researcher" can give these texts an "unbiased assessment," one which seeks "coherence" rather than one leading to "intolerance and shallowness." The authoritative scriptures of various religions are fair game for the philosopher of religion who may find in them things undreamed of by the dogmaticians. This is in effect a manifesto for the general orientation of Schelling's lectures on mythology and revelation. (Hegel's philosophy of religion, to be sure in its own way, is also an example of this new approach to the use of scriptural sources.) Schelling himself had already begun with his Old Testament explorations in *Ages*. Here he takes up the mythology and cult of Samothrace, which he links, through supposed Phoenician origins, with the same set of ideas. Actually the link is found in his own ontology, which serves to articulate the historical materials both in *Ages* and in *The Deities of Samothrace*.

4. Historical Sources and
Scholarship Influencing Schelling's Interpretation

The historical evidence upon which Schelling draws is almost exclusively literary. It consists primarily of reports of ancient authors regarding the beliefs and practices of Samothrace, and secondarily of collateral texts from the Greek and other cultures illustrating elements which he believes parallel, or constitute the source of, the Samothracian elements. Because this study is principally concerned with Schelling's own philosophical position, I will not in most instances pause to provide background information about the numerous authors and sources which he cites to make geographical, historical, and literary points. Among those he draws upon most frequently are the Homeric Hymns, Strabo, Diodorus Siculus, Herodotus, Varro, Pliny, Plutarch, Cicero, Sanchuniaton, Ovid, Clement of Alexandria and Eusebius. Information about them, as well as about some of the more obscure classical names and terms, can be found readily in a good dictionary of classical antiquity.

Schelling subscribes to a Phoenician source for the Cabiri, and is especially interested in texts which speculate on the origins of the

Samothracian cult. He evaluates the Scholia Parisina to Apollonius of Rhodes (3rd century B. C.), *Argonautica* 1.917 as:

> A single account, preserved by exceptional luck, which appears to have contained the authentic chronological sequence and order of descent of the Samothracian gods, together with the true names originally ascribed to them. (349)

The scholiast attributes to Mnaseas, the third-century traveller, this report of the names and equivalences of the first three Cabiri: Axieros (Demeter); Axiokersa (Persephone); Axiokersos (Hades). The scholiast says some people add a fourth deity, Casmilus (Hermes, according to Dionysodorus). Schelling adopts this list of names and equivalences as the basis of his own interpretation.[11]

Schelling believes that the Pelasgians, a people who came to Greece in prehistoric times, were responsible for the introduction of the Cabiri cult to Samothrace. In fact, it was popular in Schelling's day (especially under Creuzer's influence) to attribute the formative power of ancient Greek culture to the Pelasgians (363f.). Herodotus attests to this role of the Pelasgians, but arouses Schelling's displeasure when he states that they learned the names of the Cabiri in Egypt, hence the Cabiri are of Egyptian origin (*History,* II, 49 - 52). In a sustained discussion of the issue, Schelling rejects Herodotus' reasoning and, in keeping with his theory of the Phoenician origin of the Samothracian cult, argues that the Cabiri-like Egyptian pygmy deities of Herodotus' account probably themselves derived from Phoenician protector deities (363f.).[12]

Schelling's position is also shaped in various ways by his positive and negative reactions to modern scholars. Seven who are mentioned explicitly in the text and notes of *The Deities of Samothrace* translated here need to be identified briefly.

Mentioned only in passing (365) is Georg Agricola (1490 - 1555), a classicist and early scientist known as "the father of minerology." A specialist in metals and mining, he wrote a twelve-part systematic work, *De re metallica.* Schelling cites in his note 104 (in a part not translated here) a passage from the treatise *De Animantibus subterraneis* (from the twelfth book) which describes dwarfs or gnomes who reportedly live in the mountains and work with stone and metals, the "little mountain men" of popular legend which Agricola identifies with the Greek *Cobalos.*

Schelling makes important references to three scholars from the seventeenth and eighteenth centuries whose work was already quite old in his day. Gerhard Johann Vossius (1577 - 1649) was a German classical scholar and theologian, one of the first to examine both Christian dogmas and pagan religions from an historical perspective in his *Historia Pelagiana . . .*(1618), *De Theologia Gentili* (1642), and *Dissertationis Tres de Tribus Symbolis . . .* (1642). A Calvinist whose father had been forced by persecution to emigrate from Germany to the Netherlands, Vossius himself was accused of Arminian sympathies due to his critical and historical approach to the study of doctrine.

His systematic assumption was that the content of pagan religions, specifically the gods of the Greeks and Romans, was produced from the dim consciousness of God possessed by the fallen human race and was therefore an unwitting imitation of biblical revelation. To sustain this position he proposed a number of supposed etymological relations between Hebrew and Graeco-Roman terms and names, hypotheses which most modern scholars regard as unfounded and extravagant speculation. Schelling respectfully mentions Vossius together with Bochart (362), while at the same time rejecting their shared view (which runs counter to his own) that Greek mythology is only a derivative and distorted form of the original biblical revelation.

Samuel Bochart (1599 - 1667) was a French Protestant scholar and Orientalist who concentrated on biblical history and on the Phoenician language. He agreed substantially with Vossius on the historical priority of Hebrew religion and endeavored to find Phoenician origins for a great many terms and practices in a variety of languages and cultures. His major work was the *Geographiae sacrae* in two parts. Part one, *Phaleg seu de dispersione gentium*. . . (1646), traces the genealogies of all peoples and the origins of all ancient mythologies from the history of Noah and his sons. Part two, *Chanaan seu de coloniis et sermone Phoenicum* (1651), traces the historical expansion of Phoenician culture and argues for the scholarly recognition of numerous vestiges of the Phoenician language in Greek and Latin. Because the *Geographiae sacrae* was an influential work Bochart enjoyed a great reputation in his day. He also wrote *Hierozoicon*. . .(1663) in two volumes, a study of the animals mentioned in the Bible. Bochart, even more so than Vossius, was later discounted as a coiner of false etymologies. It is easily understandable that he appeals to Schelling because the two share a similar concern to find linguistic parallels between Greek and Phoenician-Hebraic sources, although Schelling also can be quite critical of Bochart's work (cf. note 29 to p. 351).

William Warburton (1698 - 1779) was an Anglican bishop and a literary critic whose most famous book was *The Divine Legation of Moses Demonstrated, on the Principles of a Religious Deist*. . . , in two volumes (1737 - 1741). (His name is misprinted as "Warbuton" in the German text.) Warburton turned the tables on the free-thinkers who held that the religious promise of reward and punishment is evidence that religion is a human contrivance designed to provide sanctions for human law in civil society. He argued that the notable absence of such promises in the Mosaic revelation should then be taken as evidence of its divine origin. Warburton also taught that monotheism was the primordial religion of the human race. Polytheistic mythology arose when priests drew a sharp distinction between an elite understanding (monotheism) and a means of teaching adapted to the masses (polytheism). Hence the mystery cults of antiquity developed with esoteric and exoteric aspects. The elite understood their mythologies as allegories of monotheism, the masses (who were also initiates) understood them literally and polytheistically. The poets perpetuated the myths as literal accounts because they lacked the elite understanding possessed by the priests. Schelling severely criticized Warburton's interpretation of the mysteries (361f.) because the old theory of a primordial monotheism runs directly counter to his own conception of the revelation and self-development of the divine in history.

The remaining three scholars requiring identification were all contemporaries of Schelling. Guillaume . . . baron de Sainte-Croix (1746 - 1809), a French antiquarian, was the author of *Examen critique des historiens d'Alexandre* (1772), and of the major and influential work, *Memoires pour servir à l'Histoire de la religion secrète des anciens peuples; où recherches historiques et critiques sur les mystères du paganisme*(1784). Schelling's references to Sainte-Croix in the notes are frequent, sometimes with criticism and sometimes with approval. He definitely rejects Sainte-Croix's thesis that the mystery religions all originated in Egypt. But he cites him (361) in support of his own rebuttal of Warburton.

Joergen Zoëga (1755 - 1809) was an Egyptologist and archaeologist. Schelling cites his *De origine et usu obeliscorum* (1797) and evidently is acquainted with his other works on ancient art and Coptic manuscripts. Schelling respects Zoëga's technical skill as an antiquarian but objects sharply to his attempted derivation of the Samothracian deities from the Egyptian religion (350). His more general work, *Vorlesungen über die Griechische Mythologie* (1817) was published subsequently to *The Deities of Samothrace*.

By far the greatest influence upon Schelling came from Georg Friedrich Creuzer (1771 - 1858), a professor of philology and ancient history at Heidelberg. Among his initial works was a treatise linking Dionysiac religon to Oriental sources: *Dionysus s. Commentationes academicae de rerum Bacchicarum Orphicarumque originibus et causis (1809)*. His *Symbolik und Mythologie der alten Völker, besonders der Griechen,* published in four volumes (1810 - 1812), was obviously devoured by Schelling and is the evident source for two of the main themes in *The Deities of Samothrace*.

First, Creuzer held that the great literary and religious products of the early Greeks, namely the mythologies of Homer and Hesiod, came to Greece from the Orient as transmitted by the Pelasgians. This thesis Schelling apparently adopted directly from Creuzer. But Creuzer also believed that the primitive Pelasgians must have been tutored in such matters by others wiser than they. Because he was committed to the view that India was the source of Greek religion and philosophy, he hypothesized that missionary priests from India must have tutored the Pelasgians at a crucial period in their history. Schelling, who links Samothracian religion with Phoenician sources, does not subscribe to this additional aspect of the Pelasgian hypothesis. Second, Creuzer argued that one can therefore find in ancient Greek religion the remains of the symbols of the most ancient revelation. Here we see a powerful stimulus to Schelling's belief that the primordial religious system of humanity could be unearthed through such research (349 and note 90 to p. 362), although it would not necessarily be a form of Hinduism as Creuzer supposed. One can therefore well imagine how Schelling's intention of demonstrating the application of his speculative conception of God to data from the history of religion and mythology crystallized under the influence of Creuzer's ideas into this treatise on the Samothracian cult, as an exploratory first step in a philosophy of mythology and revelation.

Schelling's most severe criticism of Creuzer in *The Deities of Samothrace* occurs in note 74 to p. 358, in his critique of emanation theories. Creuzer is credited with showing definitively that Axieros-Ceres is the first deity in the Samothracian series. (The point that they constitute a sequence, not just a collection, of deities is also quite important.) But because of his commitment to an Indian metaphysical framework and his willingness to accept Zoëga's equation of Axieros with the highest of the Egyptian gods, Creuzer wrongly teaches that the Samothracian deities form a descending series, hence disclose an emanation theology. This point leads us to Creuzer's theory on the relation of symbol to myth, which Schelling was to oppose in his later writings.

In one respect Creuzer was a key spokesman for the Romantic movement's view that religious myth and symbolism are not just dispensable products of primitive ignorance, but instead are profound and spiritual functions of human consciousness. What aroused the opposition of other Romantics was the way in which Creuzer relegated myth to a secondary status. In his view a symbol is a form of divine manifestation, a sign which both reveals and conceals something which cannot be given direct conceptual expression. The symbol binds the divine itself and the transient sign together in a unity; it is produced directly by the gods when revealing themselves. Myth, on the contrary, is a second-hand representation or narration which is about the gods, an interpretation geared to the understanding of a general audience. Not only did Creuzer offend the conviction of other Romantics that myth is a direct spiritual expression, by demoting it to a kind of allegorical status, but he also advanced his own version of the original monotheism hypothesis. He held that symbols disclose a monotheistic revelation, whereas the myths in which they became re-expressed teach polytheism. The consequence of this view is an esoteric-exoteric dichotomy somewhat like that proposed by Warburton. Schelling stands firmly opposed both to emanation theories and to the hypothesis of original monotheism, and he also rejects (more forcefully in his later thought) such attempts to regard mythology as allegory.

Schelling seized upon some of Creuzer's key ideas at an opportune time when they still seemed fresh and before they were criticized by other classical scholars. Gottfried Hermann (1772 - 1848), in *De mythologia Graecorum antiquissima dissertatio* (1817) and *Ueber das Wesen und die Behandlung der Mythologie: Ein Brief an Herrn Hofrath Creuzer* (1819), followed Creuzer's general schema but disagreed on the crucial point of the purported profundity of mythology, regarding it instead as rather naive in its content. Johann Heinrich Voss (1751 - 1826) argued in his *Antisymbolik* (1824 - 1826) that the gods of mythology represent forces of nature and have no hidden significance. Widely influential was the broadside of ridicule directed at the Greek mysteries by Christian August Lobeck (1781 - 1860) in his *Aglaophamus sive de theologiae mysticae Graecorum causis* (1829). More weighty was the critique of Karl Otfried Müller (1797 - 1840), *Prolegomena zu einer Wissenschaftliche Mythologie . . .* (1825). Müller argued that myths change over time in accord with changes in the culture. Hence one cannot simply "intuit" the essence of a myth, especially not from a late version. Instead one must engage in elaborate historical study of a given mythological tradition, being especially cautious with etymological analyses.

In light of all this criticism of Creuzer, some of it well-founded and some mis-directed, and also for a number of other reasons (such as later archaeological work), the historical basis of *The Deities of Samothrace* looks shaky from a modern perspective. But the main focus of this study is on its place in the development of Schelling's own categories for interpreting myth and religion. So let us turn to his text, and then proceed to the task of its philosophical interpretation.

5. Remarks on the Translation

The translation has been made from the text and notes as they appear in the Schröter edition of Schelling's collected works, which is a rearranged photographic reproduction of the pages as they stand in the K. F. A. Schelling edition. Because it is standard practice to identify passages according to the earlier collection (Schröter provides the corresponding pagination at the top of each page in his edition), I have placed in the translation of the text (but not of the notes) the page numbers of the K. F. A. Schelling edition, to indicate the approximate points at which new pages commence.

The printed German text of this address has no paragraph divisions. However there are consecutive Arabic numerals in the margins at points where a shift in subject occurs. Since these are likely intended as indications of paragraphs, I have begun new paragraphs at these points. The use of parentheses and square brackets in the translation corresponds exactly to the occurrence of these signs in the original. I have employed angle brackets (〈 〉) to enclose my own additions, which include the following: my summaries of some lengthy materials omitted from translated notes; occasional words introduced in the interest of clarity or style, having no close equivalents in Schelling's German; a few German words reproduced after their translated equivalents. Italics is used only for words italicized by Schelling in the original through the use of different type or by the device in German of widely separating the letters, and for German words I have reproduced within angle brackets. In a few instances an obviously foreign word such as "Elohim" is printed in Gothic type as is the text itself. These words I have not italicized. Schelling frequently varies the spelling of certain names and technical terms derived from ancient languages, even when no specific linguistic comparison is at issue, as his references switch from one ancient source to another. The translation follows his shifts in spelling, rather than attempting to impose an artificial uniformity which in some cases would obscure the nature of his argument. The only exception is the case of certain names which Schelling routinely in Gothic type spells with an initial "K." In passages where no etymological issue is under discussion I have spelled these names with a "C" ("Cabiri," "Cadmus," "Corybants," and so forth) because these are the forms familiar to English language readers. I have used my own judgment in deciding where to employ quotation marks in the English translation, for the text makes no use of them although Schelling's notes do. In a few instances Schelling capitalizes the first letter of *"ein"* and its derivatives where the form is adjectival or adverbial, and also does this for several other words where an initial capital is ordinarily unexpected. He presumably makes these capitalizations for special emphasis, or to indicate an unusual usage such as "the One" — *das Eine.* Capitalization of these words in English translation seems obtrusive and unnecessary for the most part. Therefore it has been dropped except in references to "the One" and several other spots where such emphasis seemed especially desirable.

Schelling's notes present a formidable problem. They consist chiefly of detailed philological and historical remarks and citations of classical authors, much of this material being in a variety of ancient languages. Where a note or part of a note bears in an important way on Schelling's argument or discloses a particularly interesting assessment of his scholarly predecessors or contemporaries I have translated or summarized that material. These notes appear at the conclusion of the text proper. The rest has been omitted. Schelling places his footnote numbers on the line, within parentheses. I follow the same practice, but only those numbers appear for which I have chosen to include the note. Occasionally I summarize the import of a note or part of a note without actually translating. In all cases my own words within the translation of Schelling's notes appear within angle brackets. Translator's footnotes are identified in the text in the conventional way and are placed at the end of Part Two. In a few instances Schelling's citation of classical texts in now obsolete editions has been replaced with altered or fuller citations of the texts as they may be located in more recent editions. Schelling cites many classical authors and makes passing references to numerous characters and incidents in ancient literature and history, sometimes without elaboration in his notes. The translator's notes remark on very few of these points, and only where it seems especially desirable to do so. Of necessity Greek and Hebrew words which Schelling places in his notes in the original alphabets have had to be transliterated for this printing. Schelling sometimes transliterates Hebrew words himself, a few times immediately following their presentation in the Hebrew alphabet. In order to distinguish his transliteration from mine, in the translation of his notes I always place an asterisk after those Hebrew words or phrases which I have transliterated from the Hebrew script as presented by Schelling.

In translating I have attempted to be as literal as possible, although I have sometimes rearranged clauses and subdivided long sentences in the interest of English style. I hope the resulting translation adequately captures Schelling's meaning. I know all too well that it sometimes gets tangled in the intricacies of his complex style, while failing to convey the elegance with which he writes.

Notes to Part One

[1]*Ueber die Gottheiten von Samothrake,* Stuttgart and Tübingen: J. G. Cotta'schen Buchhandlung, 1815. The text and notes appear in: K. F. A. Schelling, editor, *Friedrich Wilhelm Joseph von Schellings sämmtliche Werke* (14 vols.; Stuttgart and Augsburg: J. G. Cotta'scher Verlag, 1856-61), vol. 8, pages 345-422. It is also found in: Manfred Schröter, editor, *Schellings Werke, Nach der Original Ausgabe in neuer Anordnung* (6 vols. and 6 supplementary vols.; Munich: C. H. Beck and R. Oldenbourg, 1927-1959), the text being in vol. 4, pages 721-45, and the notes in supplementary vol. 4, pages 3-55. Hereafter supplementary volumes are indicated by an "s" before the volume number, for example "s4."

[2]*Philosophische Untersuchungen über das Wesen der menschlichen Freiheit und die damit zusammenhängenden Gegenstände* (1809), 7, 331-416 (4, 223-308). (For works other than *The Deities of Samothrace* I follow the customary practice of giving the reference in the K. F. A. Schelling edition first, followed by the Schröter edition reference in parentheses.) There is an English translation by James Gutmann, *Schelling: Of Human Freedom* (Chicago: Open Court, 1936).

[3]Major components of the ontology were new to Schelling. Those elements derived from Boehme, Schelling recast in a form much improved in sophistication and clarity of presentation. An account of Schelling's systematic thought of 1809-1815, in its genesis and detail, may be found in my forthcoming book, *The Later Philosophy of Schelling: The Influence of Boehme on the Works of 1809-1815* (Lewisburg, Pa.: Bucknell University Press, 1976).

[4]*Stuttgarter Privatvorlesungen* (1810), 7, 417-84 (4, 309-76). There is no complete English translation, but key passages have been translated in my book, cited in the preceding note.

[5]*F. W. J. Schellings Denkmal der Schrift von den göttlichen Dingen etc. des Herrn Friedrich Heinrich Jacobi und der ihm in derselben gemachten Beschuldigung eines absichtlich täuschenden, Lüge rendenden Atheismus* (1812), 8, 19-136 (4, 395-512).

[6] Schelling published Eschenmayer's criticism and his own response in a new periodical he was editing, and both appear together in his collected works under the title, *Aus der Allgemeinen Zeitschrift von Deutschen für Deutsche* (1813), 8, 137-93 (4, 513-69).

[7]*Die Weltalter.* The text printed in the collected works, 8, 195-344 (4, 571-720), was selected by the editor as the latest and fullest of several available manuscripts, and dated 1815. It has been translated into English by Frederick de Wolfe Bolman, Jr., *Schelling: The Ages of the World* (New York: Columbia University Press, 1942). Schröter has published as a *"Nachlassband"* to his edition of the collected works materials he had copied from unpublished manuscripts of *Ages* just prior to their destruction by bombing in 1944, consisting of the earlier texts of 1811 and 1813 plus other fragments: *Die Weltalter: Fragmente, In den Urfassungen von 1811 und 1813,* ed. by

Manfred Schröter (Munich: C. H. Beck'sche Verlagsbuchhandlung, 1946). Thus we see that Schelling worked on various versions of *Ages* from 1811-1815 but never got it in a publishable form satisfactory to him. Perhaps he sensed its incompleteness without the historical studies that were to follow.

⁸The topic of mythology was not entirely new to Schelling in 1815. The writings of his student days include his Master's dissertation on the biblical story of the fall, *Antiquissimi de prima malorum humanorum origine. . .* (1792), 1, 1-40 (sl, 1-40), and *Ueber Mythen, historische Sagen und Philosopheme der ältesten Welt* (1793), 1, 41-83 (1, 1-43).

⁹The reader is referred to the bibliograpy at the conclusion of this study for sources of information about archaeological discoveries and the status of scholarship on Samothrace since the time of Schelling's treatise. Schelling's account of the Samothracian deities (collectively called "the Cabiri") and cult is generally correct on the following points. The Cabiri were essentially fertility gods, worshipped in secret rites or mysteries to which men and women could be admitted by receiving the initiation. (Schelling does not stress the sexual factor, and seems not as aware of the explicitly phallic symbolism in the rites as are modern scholars.) The Cabiri offered protection from misfortunes and sanctuary for those committing certain offenses, and were especially beneficial to mariners. The rites upheld high moral standards for initiation, and attracted many prominent persons in the early Hellenistic Age. The theory of a Phoenician origin for the Cabiri, to which Schelling subscribes, is no longer generally accepted. The majority of scholars now think that the Cabiri, who also came to be worshipped among the Greeks on Lemnos, and in Macedonia and Boeotia, probably derived from Phrygia. Schelling's interpretation of the four main deities also differs somewhat from current views.

¹⁰The extended remarks on pages 347-49 credit the Samothracian cult with introducing to the Greek world belief in an afterlife, and with exerting a positive moral and intellectual force on the famous persons of antiquity (Pythagoras, Philip of Macedon, et al) who came there for initiation. (References to Schelling's text cite page numbers of the edition by his son. Schröter supplies the same numbers at the tops of pages in his edition, and they appear in the text of my translation. References to Schelling's notes cite both the note number and the K. F. A. Schelling edition pagination on which the citation, but not the note itself, appears. These citations are placed in parentheses, so as not to multiply footnotes unnecessarily).

¹¹Schelling at this point disregards the next sentences of the scholia, which cite other ancient sources according to which the Cabiri consisted of two male deities, who were brought from Phrygia. (Later, in note 112, to p. 366, he dismisses the report of two Cabiri, attributed to Athenion, as not based on the reporter's actual knowledge.) He argues (note 22 to p. 349) that the first three equivalences derive from Mnaseas himself, not from the scholiast. (These materials from notes 22 and 112 are not included in the translation which follows).

¹²To sustain his argument that his own interpretation of the natures of the Cabiri is compatible with the theory of their Phoenician origin, he cites in notes 44 and 45 (to p. 354) two obscure references purporting to give "fragments of Phoenician cosmogony": Eusebius' *Praeparatio Evangelica* 2.10 (4th century A. D.) and a sentence from Damascius' *Dubitationes et solutiones de primis principiis* (6th century A. D.) regarding the Sidonians' view of time. He also draws on Varro (via Augustine, *City of God,* Book 7) to buttress his triadic arrangement of the deities.

Part Two

The Deities of Samothrace

1. Text

|347| The island of Samothrace rises from the northern part of the Aegean Sea. Evidently from the beginning it was called "Samos," but later "the Thracian Samos" to differentiate it from the Samos of the Ionian Sea and because of the proximity of Thrace. Ancient geographers surmised that great convulsions of nature afflicted these regions even up to human times. It may be that the waters of the Black Sea, raised simply by flooding, first broke through the Thracian Strait and then through the Hellespont. Or that the [more extreme] force of a subterranean volcano altered the level of the waters. The oldest Samothracian stories, transmuted into monuments exhibited in commemoration, preserved an account of this event, and from that time on they fostered the reverence and patronage of the native gods (4). The ever-present awe of a vast and mighty nature intensified the terrors of these memories. The forested, almost inaccessible island forms only a single continuous mountain chain. From its highest peak during the Trojan War Poseidon surveyed the entire mountain range of Ida, Priam's city, and the Danaean fleet (7).

A mysterious polytheism was established there in indeterminable antiquity. If the many-splendored Ionian Samos be renowned for the divinely esteemed man ⟨Pythagoras⟩ who first devised a community aiming for a higher humanity, even so the unprepossessing Thracian Samos is more splendid in human history due to the cult of the Cabiri, the most ancient in all of Greece. With it there dawned in this region the first light of a higher and finer knowledge, which evidently perished not prior to, but along with, the ancient |348| belief itself. Together with the secret history of the gods, Greece first received from the forests of Samothrace the belief in a future life. According to the prevailing view, the persons initiated there became better and happier in both life and death. A refuge from misfortune, even from crime so far as it admitted of propitiation through confession and purification, Samothracian practice in both earlier and later times mitigated the savagery of human emotion. It is no wonder that the name of the sacred island became intertwined with all that the oldest histories preserved as venerable and

15

famous. Iasion and Dardanus, Orpheus and the Argonauts, even Hercules and Ulysses, are said to have taken part in the secret rites established there and to have undergone the initiation. A report both plausible and noteworthy names Pythagoras among those who sought and found wisdom there. Philip of Macedon and the mother of Alexander the Great, Olympia, while still a child, first met at the orgies of the Cabiri. Perhaps this fact was not without influence on the future destiny of their son. Even the Roman rule spared the freedom and the ancient, evidently theocratic, government of Samothrace. Divested of his realm, there the last Macedonian king (Perseus) sought asylum, from which he was driven out not by the power of the already arrogantly ruling Romans, but by the holiness of the place itself and the murder perpetrated on his own commander-in-chief. Had he not been driven back by a northerly gale, the noble Germanicus would have received the initiation there shortly before his end. Authors from the later Empire take pleasure in mentioning the Samothracian sanctuaries with lasting respect. And even if the antiquarian did not expect to discover in the continuing sacred rites features from the portrait of the old Samothracian cult, still, owing to other clues, one would be able to pursue its continuation up to the end of the second, even into the third, century of the Christian era. Now that more than ever public attention is again directed to ancient Greece, if this almost forgotten island would be investigated thoroughly like the others perhaps |349| the yield of such research would not be the value of the art works, as in that incomparable discovery on Aegina,[1] but instead monuments of the most ancient belief, even more important than the former for the entire history of our species.

In that light, after so many analyses yet another examination of this secret cult of the gods seems of value, especially for the following reasons. The significance of the individual deities is still concealed in darkness. It is true that more than one author mentions their Greek names. We know that Demeter, Dionysos, Hermes, and even Zeus were revered as Cabiri. But for us these are mere names which leave a lingering doubt whether the Samothracian gods were only somewhat similar and comparable to those familiar deities, or were one with them in fact and in basic idea. It is just as uncertain how these gods, as objects of the secret doctrine, differ from the same gods in the public cult and general belief. Yet only this related information can provide a fundamental explanation of the meaning of the Samothracian doctrine, of the actual system lying at its foundation. A single account, preserved by exceptional luck (21), appears to have contained the authentic chronological sequence and order of descent of the Samothracian gods, together with the true names originally ascribed to them. Therefore, it seems proper that *this* lay the foundation of all inquiries.

The passage of the Greek commentator to whom we are indebted for the preservation of this account reads as follows. "In Samothrace one receives the initiation of the Cabiri. Mnaseas says they are three in number: Axieros,

Axiokersa, Axiokersos, and that Axieros is Demeter, Axiokersa Persephone, and Axiokersos Hades. Some even add a fourth, called Kasmilos, which is Hermes as Dionysodoros explains." This source places an evident importance on the sequence of these personalities, on the number belonging to each one. Because it contains the original names it also provides the occasion for comparison and for the investigation of the underlying concept of each deity. For it seems perilous, even almost outrageous, to wish to take the names from the ancient historian, |350| but to investigate the meaning from other, wholly independent, sources. It is entirely reasonable to agree that whoever knew the secret names also was not unaware of their general significance. It is recognized that they are not Hellenic, that, in the Greek expression, they are of "barbarian" origin. To which language and people they originally belonged is a question capable of a purely linguistic resolution independent of any historical supposition. It was natural for the diligent Zoëga,[2] who spent his whole life buried in Egyptological research, to trace the roots of these names in the dubious remnants of the Old Egyptian language. But when through his research he brought to light characteristic meanings of the most general and indeterminate sort rather than definite, specific personalities, or when Axieros is supposed to signify the almighty and Kasmilos the completely wise, then through such explanantions the very derivation already becomes suspect. It remains uncertain whether a more satisfactory conclusion is possible from Indian vocabulary. We believed it necessary to set out again on another path than that taken by previous investigators.

From whatever people the names and the gods designated by them originally may have come, surely they were predominantly a maritime people. For it is the most universal belief that those deities were especially helpful and salutary to searfarers. The origin and perpetuation of this belief scarcely admits of any other explanation than that they were first known as the gods of a people venturing out to sea, therefore apparently favored (by them). How natural in those still-dangerous seas for far-sailing foreigners, frequently long detained from the business of trade by storms and gales off these islands, to wish to find again and worship the gods of the homeland; with the consequence that these very ships which brought incense, purple dye and ivory there also transplanted their gods and sanctuaries on the Greek coast and islands. Of such a people in those ancient times we know only the Phoenicians, whose long-extended operations and control, indeed whose |351| settlements in that region, historically cannot be denied. Add to this the declaration by Herodotus that the Egyptian Cabiri would have been similar in form to the tutelary gods of the Phoenicians whose insignia they placed on the prows of their ships. Consequently if Samothrace received its gods either indirectly or directly from the Phoenician sailors, and if in all probability also the names as well as the gods were from this people, then that is the strongest reason to trace the meaning of those names in Phoenician or Hebraic linguistic roots. It doesn't matter which, due to the incontestable unity of both languages. For we require no proof and scarcely any reminder that in the East, where people's given names are meaningful, the names of gods are meaningful, too.

Thus we set foot upon that hazardous path of philology which is concerned with investigation of the origin and derivation of names or words, aware of what the cautious expert is accustomed to say of its difficulty and thanklessness, and apprised of the condemnation which the less thoughtful in general pronounce upon it. But every investigation is commendable in itself; only the method and the procedure make the difference. It may have been the case that, in a time when everyone readily believed himself equal to every task, a new frenzy of linguistic derivations struggled to produce everything from everything, and mixed all things together in a crazy manner even in the old stories of the gods. However, the inquiry into the origin and derivation of words will always remain the noblest branch of linguistic research when not pursued blindly, but skillfully and according to its appropriate rules (29).

We can pass over in silence the common prefix of the first three deities as not being significant for the special nature of each. But according to the literal translation the first name, Axieros, in the Phoenician dialect can not very well mean other than [in the first instance] "hunger," "poverty," and in consequence "yearning," "seeking" (31). At first glance this explanation might seem strange, but it is clear upon deeper reflection [and is immediately |352| intelligible of itself, so soon as one notes that according to the intention of the ancient historian Axieros must be regarded as the first being (*Wesen*), commencing all]. We will not rest content with the general point that an absolutely *first* being, even though in itself abundant fullness, must seem to itself as the most extreme poverty, the greatest need insofar as it has *nothing* to which it can communicate itself. It is not merely that in the concept of *every* beginning lies the concept of a lack (32). We hasten to recall the specific case of that Platonic Penia who, by uniting herself with Abundance, becomes the mother of Eros.[3] It is true that in the Greek version, which allows the most ancient deities to be born again in the [later] realm of Zeus, this Penia appears at the banquet of the other gods. But doubtless here, as in other instances, Plato merely employs freely an already-existing tale. The raw material of his narrative is a fragment of that age-old doctrine according to which Eros is the first of the gods to proceed out of the world-egg, whereas before it there is only the night bearing the egg. For it was the teaching of all peoples who counted time by nights that the *night* is the most primordial of things in all of nature, although it is a misrepresentation if one also regards this first being as the highest. But what is the essence of night, if not lack, need, and longing? For this night is not darkness, not the enemy of the light, but it is the nature looking forward to the light, the night longing for it, eager to receive it. Another image of that first nature, whose whole essence is desire and passion, appears in the consuming fire which so to speak is itself nothing, is in essence only a hunger drawing everything into itself. Hence the ancient precept: fire is the most inward, therefore also the oldest; through the subduing of fire everything first began to be a world. Thus it was that Hestia came to be revered as the oldest [first] of beings, and the concepts of Ceres and Proserpina, the most ancient deities, became intertwined with that of Hestia. The feminine character of this many-named being points to the concepts of longing and of yearning |353| desire, as do all names of the first nature either obscurely or clearly; so especially the nature of Ceres, whom the ancient historian interpreted as the first Samothracian deity, arises wholly as yearning passion ⟨[*Sehn-*] *Sucht*⟩. In first manifesting herself she replies to the daughters of Celeus, "I am Deo," that is, "the one afflicted with yearning," "the pining one," a meaning which would require a context if it could not vindicate itself in philology. As Isis in seeking the lost god, so Ceres in seeking her lost daughter becomes wholly the seeking one. Yet the initial foundation of the concept lies deeper. [The first is also the lowest.] Everything lowest, beneath which there is nothing further, can only be seeking, a nature which is not insofar as it merely strives to be. Thus in the Egyptian view Ceres is ruler of the dead, whose general status is conceived as a condition of incapacity and impotent striving for reality. The underworld itself is called "the covetous, the avaricious," Dis or Amenthes. From antiquity on the Athenians called the departed ones "Demetrian," because they thought of those persons separated from the body and from the external world as being transposed into a condition of sheer longing, for the same reason that the shades were called in the Hebrew language, "the seeking ones," "the desiring ones." But no one hitherto uses the words of that less profound than clever Roman poet ⟨Ovid⟩, "No more does Hunger go together with Ceres," sufficiently to remember that we know not only of a fruit-bearing Ceres, but also of a Ceres-Erinys; and as the Erinyes in general belong to the more ancient deities, so precisely the fearful Ceres is the older ⟨form⟩. For the burning desire must precede the satisfied desire, and the greatest receptivity, thus consuming hunger, must precede the abundant fullness of fecundity. Its full significance is best conveyed in the punishment of Erysichthon, whom the angry Ceres inflicts with insatiably ravenous hunger. For the serious scholar is familiar with the notion that that person who has been overwhelmed by their favor the gods punish by banishment into just that state. Therefore in the underworld the uninitiated suffer the specific punishment that they ceaselessly strive to fill an unfillable vessel. |354| These references could appear adequate for establishing the given explanation. Nevertheless we believe it can be brought nearer to certainty. Diverse fragments of the Phoenician cosmogony have been preserved for us. One of them locates time above all the gods, which time itself has no number because it is the common context and bearer of all numbers; next to it, however, and therefore as the first number, it mentions the wistful longing (*die schmachtende Sehnsucht*)[4] (44). Another fragment of Phoenician cosmogony, which obviously bears the mark of greater antiquity, expresses itself as follows. First there was the breathing of a dark atmosphere and a turbid chaos, in itself entirely boundless. But when the spirit of love was kindled in the presence of the special beginning, and a contraction (of the two) resulted, this bond was called longing and it was the beginning of the creation of all things (45). Here the beginning was established in a flaming passion directed toward itself, a self-seeking; the bond constituted thereby is once again longing, only now in embodied form, and the inducement for the creation of all things. Therefore the representation of longing as the beginning, as first ground of creation, was indigenous to Phoenician cosmogony. But was this also the case for Samothrace? The answer is provided by a text of Pliny, which cites among the sculptures by Skopas, a Venus, a Phaëton, that is, longing, and a Pothos,[5] deities (he adds) which were honored in Samothrace with the most sacred rites. Thus it is assured that there was one among the Samothracian deities to which the concept of longing was linked. We know all the Samothracian deities with considerable certainty. But there is none to which yearning longing would be so characteristic, so completely suited, as that one which the ancient historian identifies with Demeter, in short the one named Axieros (47). Thereby we believe the explanation given provides that degree of certainty possible in such inquiries.

Regarding the following |355| names of the second and third personalities, Axiokersa and Axiokersos, one might well be astonished above all at the fact that none of the preceding investigators has noticed in them the mark of the very old root of the Ceres-name, for in this context everything points to the cult and doctrine of Ceres. Actually, according to another dialect, Kersa is just the same as Ceres (in the archaic pronunciation, Keres). And because according to the previously proven meaning of Axieros there is no doubt that Axiokersa is Persephone, so this name serves merely as a new verification of the otherwise known fact that Proserpina is just Ceres, the daughter just the mother in another form, and that even their names were interchanged, as often their images (49). Demeter as well as Persephone can be called "magic" or "sorceress" (for this is what the words mean). For, as [the pining for reality, as] the hunger for being which we recognize as the most inward aspect of all of [longing-filled] nature, Ceres is the moving power through whose ceaseless attraction everything, as if by magic, is brought from the primal indeterminateness to actuality or formation. However the originally formless deity, revered in her temple at Rome as Vesta without images and in the pure flame, takes on form in Persephone, and this one first actually becomes the living magic, at once the agent and the form to which the inscrutable magic is linked. To be brief about this significance let us use Creuzer's scholarly classification, which admits as highest hardly any other unifying concept than that of sorceress, which moreover can include even that of the artiste. [According to the expression of the ancients] Persephone is a sorceress, as the initial beginning of future bodily existence, as the one who weaves this garment of mortality and generates the deception of the senses, but most generally as the first link of that chain extending from the depths to the heights, binding together beginning and end (52). Persephone is even called

"Maja," a name which reminds us more than a little of magic. Artemis would also be what Persephone (was), as Aeschylus is supposed to have rumored, and Artemis is also called |356| sorceress according to the most natural derivation. But the concept of magic generally lies at the basis of *all* female deities. As the mythology of the Old Germans, related to that of Samothrace though more inward, as would be expected, associates Freya with Othin and ascribes mighty magical powers to both, in the same way Axiokersa and Axiokersos are linked through the common concept of magic.

Then this third form is actually none other than the one who was Osiris to the Egyptians, Dionysos to the Greeks, Othin to the Germans. It is true that the Greek historian interprets Axiokersos as Hades, and all commentators actually understand this to mean Pluto or the Stygian Jupiter. But Heraclitus earlier taught that Hades and Dionysos are the same (58); and Osiris-Dionysos is king over the departed (59) just as our German Othin, beneficent god and first bearer of good tidings, is also lord in the realm of the dead. Indisputably the blissful conviction which the esoteric doctrines imparted was *this* teaching that the *friendly* god Dionysos was Hades. Souls do not proceed downwards to the harsh subterranean Zeus, but rather upwards to the gentle god Osiris; this was the most secret meaning of the teaching that Dionysos is Hades. This is clearly shown from a text of Plutarch, as well as from that obituary so common on Roman tombstones: "Live blessed with Osiris." In this context Persephone was not the consort of Hades but instead, as Kore and Libera, was the spouse of Dionysos. Yet in public usage Hades still remained at least in possession of the name, and so now Dionysos himself is called Hades. Thus Dionysos or Osiris is Axiokersos, as surely also Axiokersa-Persephone is Isis. But it is difficult to say what the name [Axiokersos] expresses in particular, for we do not know it in its original form. Is this personality called Axiokersos simply as the husband of Axiokersa? Or is he magician in a higher sense, as the one who overcomes the magic of Persephone, tempers her harshness, subdues and exorcizes that primordial fire (for she also is fire) (64)? In any case this could be settled only through investigations which |357| are not suited to this lecture. But whatever particular meaning one gives to the name besides the general meanings, Dionysos is a magical god, whether one recalls the apparitions with which he punished the Tyrrhenian sailors, or his office as awakener of nature, as the god moderating all things, as the one who dampens and controls the desiccating fire.

Thus the first three Samothracian gods form the very same sequence and chain in which also we everywhere find Demeter, Persephone, and Dionysos. There follows the fourth figure, called "Kasmilos," more commonly "Kadmilos," and also "Camillus." Regarding this name all investigators are now to this extent agreed, that it signifies a serving god, and also that the function of the Etruscan-Roman Camillus would shed some light on it. But of which god or gods is he a servant? The no less unanimous opinion is that he is associated as servant with those gods preceding him, and indeed by the specific concept of subordination (67). But would Kadmilos or Hermes then be subordinate to Ceres, to Proserpina, to Bacchus? For it is indubitable that he is Hermes. Is Mercury, otherwise pre-eminently messenger of Zeus, the highest of the gods, called servant of these deities? Certainly he recalls Proserpina from the underworld, but only at Jupiter's bidding and not in the service of Ceres. One finds in Varro the expression: "Camillus, a god, the servant of the great gods." But of which gods he is servant is itself presupposed although not made specific, because the Cabiri deities were called "the great" without distinction. For their number is given quite definitely as seven, with which an eighth is associated. Therefore, as servant of the great gods, Camillus is not necessarily servant of those first three. But it is established that he simultaneously served the lower and the higher gods. Hence he served the former only insofar as he was the *mediator* between them and the higher, and thus himself was higher than they. Likewise this is the *most essential* concept of Hermes, to be the governing bond between the higher and lower gods. Therefore he would serve the higher and lower in a very different sense, the former as an actual servant, as an obedient instrument, but the latter |358| as a beneficent nature, exalted above them. However it is very much to be feared that the entire Samothracian system has been placed in a false light, due to the too-easily-accepted view that Kadmilos is related to the three first deities as servant. The name itself confirms that misgiving. For "Kadmilos" with the Greek ending, with the original as "Kadmiel," literally means: "he who goes before the god" (71), and again according to Oriental usage this means nothing else than "the harbinger," "the herald of the coming god." To that extent he is related to the unknown god, just as the so-called "angel of the presence" (or "countenance") is related to the Old Testament Jehovah (72). For the "presence" means the same thing as "Kadmi," namely "the front"; therefore the angel of the presence is the messenger who is likewise the forepart, that preceding the deity. Thus Kadmilos is not servant of the deities going before him, but servant of a still-future god, coming [for the first time]. Moreover the other name, no less authentic, also signifies a god following after him rather than one preceding him. "Kasmilos" does not after all name merely an "interpreter of divinity," as it is customarily rendered, but specifically one who foretells the deity, who in preceding it announces its coming. Thus the names positively point to a future god to which Kadmilos or Hermes himself, and so necessarily also the gods preceding him, relate only as subordinated, only as servant, as herald, proclaimer. Therefore from the nature of the individual personalities themselves it would be proven that neither the first, Axieros, as unity and source of gods and of the world, is at the head, nor is there contained in the Cabiri doctrine in general an emanation system in the Egyptian sense (74). Far from following in descending order, the gods succeed one another in ascending order. Axieros is certainly the first nature, but not the highest; Kadmilos is the last among the four, but the highest.

Naturally the sensible researcher has the inclination so far as possible to comprehend everything human in a humane way; therefore in researching the ancient mythology it is natural to seek a means whereby the multiplicity of divine natures may be harmonized with the humanly necessary |359| and indelible idea of the unity of god. But it is neither suitable and clear in itself to represent the diverse gods as merely emanations of One into them, as a primal power propagating itself into diverse rays (75); nor can its indeterminateness and boundlessness be compatible as well with the determinateness and sharpness of the outlines of every individual form, as also with the limited number of these forms. But it can not even be harmonized well with the human way of thinking. For whoever elevates "Once" ⟨*Einmal*⟩ to the thought of One ⟨*Ein*⟩ highest being from which all other natures are merely radiations, will scarcely direct his reverence to these radiations, not to mention that sincere emotional piety which we observe in many of the wisest and best, such as a Xenophon, who were initiated either in the mysteries or in the teaching of the philosophers. It is an entirely different matter if the various gods be not downward-proceeding, ever more self-attenuating emanations of a highest and superior deity; if instead they be gradations of a lowest power lying at the basis, which are all finally transfigured in One highest personality. Then they are as links of a chain ascending from the depths into the heights, or as rungs of a ladder, the lower of which cannot be bypassed by one who wants to climb the higher ones. Because for a human being they are mediators between him and the highest divinity, though only as messengers, proclaimers, heralds of the coming god, the worship of them acquires a lustre which even endures for the higher humanity. This fact alone explains how the honor rendered to the multiple gods strikes roots so deep and almost ineradicable, how it can maintain itself for so long. Therefore the notion of emanation seems suited neither for the interpretation of ancient mythology in general, nor for the interpretation of Samothracian mythology in particular. Here it founders on the correctly understood concept of Kadmilos.

The four Samothracian deities authentically known to us form a series ascending from below, as do numbers. Kadmilos is not subordinated to the other three, but rather stands above them. This insight at once transforms the whole sequence into one which is living and progressing, |360| and opens up for us the prospect of a further development of the series known up to the fourth number. The next question concerns the nature of that El, that god who indeed is served and proclaimed by all of the preceding deities, but chiefly and most directly by Kadmilos. It is indisputable that a new series of revelations commences with this god, through which the sequence of personalities continues up to a total of seven or eight. Yet our aim is not the complete development of this series, which requires still other means than are available to us in the Samothracian traditions. It will suffice us, so far as this is possible, to give some information about the nature of the deity [immediately] following Kadmilos.

First of all it is clear that those initial deities are the very same powers through whose action and rule the whole world chiefly was constituted; thus it is clear that they are worldly, cosmic deities. Collectively they are called Hephaestos, in no other sense than Alexander the Great declared that Parmenion would also be Alexander. Hephaestos himself is not in a sequence of Cabiri, as little as his name appears among those of the seven planets or in the circuit of the days of the week, ⟨which is⟩ the key to all systems of gods, as I hope to show someday. Taken all together these preceding deities, or as we also could say, these serving deities, are Hephaestos. The creation of Hephaestos is the world of necessity. He is that which holds the All in strict constraint. But he is [also the artistic sculptor of the Whole. He is] also that which forms the innerworldly seat of the gods, certainly of the ones higher than he himself. Therefore this is just what those serving deities do who again exhibit themselves through the fact that they are only the epiphany, preparing the revelation of the higher gods. One could say of them that they are not so much divine as they are god-producing, theurgic natures, and the whole chain presents itself more and more as theurgic. If then those preceding personalities are [inner]-worldly deities, so the god to whom they are the leader and ladder, whom Kadmilos directly serves, is the *transcendent* god, the god who rules them and thus is lord of the world, the demiurge or, in the highest |361|sense, Zeus (80). Thus in Eleusis the one who represented Hermes or Kadmilos was called the holy herald; but the highest priest, who represented the highest of the gods, was the image of the world builder and adorned as such. The Etruscan-Roman Camillus was in no sense an aide serving any priest indiscriminately; according to the explicit account of the ancient historian he was the serving boy to the priest of Jupiter, a fact not previously noted. Therefore because this one represented Zeus himself, Camillus stood in the very same relation to him in which Kadmilos of the Cabiri, in our view, stood to the highest god. The ascending series now reads as follows. The lowest is Ceres, whose essence is hunger and seeking, and who is the first and remotest origin of all actual, revealed being. The next, Proserpina, is the essence or fundamental origin of the whole visible [external] nature. Then comes Dionysos, lord of the spirit world. Over nature and the spirit world is Kadmilos or Hermes who has both subordinate to him, as well as mediating between them and the transcendent. Beyond all these is the demiurge, the god who stands free over against the world (84).

Thus the Cabiri doctrine was a system ascending from subordinate personalities or nature deities up to a highest personality ruling them all, a transcendent god. But this description is also far removed from that other contention, which Warburton first decked out and German scholars after him also found acceptable, according to which the actual secret of all the mysteries of antiquity was the doctrine of the unity of god, and indeed excluding all multiplicity in that negating sense which the current age tied to this concept. Such a contradiction between the public cult of the gods and the secret doctrine plainly would be unthinkable. As Sainte-Croix remarked, it couldn't have lasted even for a short time, much less for two thousand years, without overturning the altars, without shaking the peace of the civil society. To create with one hand and overthrow with the other, to deceive openly and enlighten in secret, to buttress the cult of the gods by laws and earnestly punish desecration while secretly |362| nourishing and encouraging unbelief: what a way to make laws! That way of thinking might perhaps suit an age accustomed to deception [yes even boasting of deception] in so many situations, but one which antiquity, so honest, sound and robust, repudiates as with one voice (87). All likelihood is rather that exactly the same thing was depicted in the mysteries as in the public cult, but only according to its concealed references, and that the former differed no more from the latter than the esoteric or akroamatic discourses of the philosophers differed from their exoteric ones. However, that so-called monotheism which is not derived from the Old or New Testaments but is perhaps Mohammedan, the conception of which in fact lies ever at the basis of those contentions, opposes all of antiquity and the finer humanity which is reflected fully in the utterances of Heraclitus, to which Plato also gives approval: "The One wise nature does not wish to be called that exclusively; it wishes the name 'Zeus'" (88)![6]

One might have ventured to give a different outcome to that admittedly fleeting comparison between Samothracian and Old Testament representations, especially as it would, if carried further, lead to deeper points of agreement. In it one could have wished to see a new confirmation of the older position composed by Gerhard Vossius, Bochart and other respectable researchers. According to them the entire mythology of heathendom is only a disfigurement of Old Testament history and the revelation that came to God's people. This is therefore taken as an outermost and final limit, beyond which no historical interpretation can venture. But what if this hypothesis itself be only arbitrary? What if already in Greek mythology (not to mention Indian and other Oriental mythologies) there emerged the remains of a knowledge, indeed even a scientific system, which goes far beyond the circle drawn by the oldest revelation known through scriptural evidences (90)? What if after all this (scriptural revelation) had not so much opened up a new stream of knowledge, but rather had taken that already opened up through an earlier (means) and confined it to a riverbed more narrow but therefore leading onward more steadily? What if, |363| after there had set in a decline and an unpreventable deterioration into polytheism, it had with the most prudent restriction retained only a portion of that original system, but yet those very features which could lead back again to a great and comprehensive whole?

Be that as it may, those comparisons at least prove that the Greek divine belief leads back to nobler sources than do Egyptian and Indian representations. If the question arises, "Which of the various mythologies stands nearer the primary source, the Egyptian and Indian, or the Greek?", the unbiased investigator would scarcely hesitate to decide in favor of the last. In the Greek fables that history of the gods, as it was created for the Greeks pre-eminently by Homer, is an innocent, almost childish fantasy which breaks the bond by which the many deities are one god, but breaks it only tentatively, in play, and with the proviso of restoring it. In the Egyptian and Indian doctrine there is a serious misconception, even unmistakably demonic, a spirit of error working as if intentionally which develops the misconception into something monstrous, indeed aweful (*Gräuelhaft*). If the Pelasgians, that prehistoric people from whom all Greek power and mastery appears to have come, had received the fundamental conceptions in a form already obscured rather than in natural innocence and freshness, then, however highly we might estimate the lively intelligence of the Greeks, these conceptions could never have unfolded in such unalloyed beauty, never preserved so truly, so guilelessly, so untrammeled in play, those profounder connections the secret magic of which still strikes even us when we allow the divine figures to hold sway before us in their full poetic and artistic independence. That bond dissolved in the play of poetry was reinstated in the solemnity of the secret doctrines. It is historically certain that these came to the Greeks from foreign parts, or from the barbarians. But why precisely from Egypt? Because Herodotus heard from the Dodonaean priestess that the Pelasgians first learned the names of the deities from Egypt? But shortly before the very same Herodotus presents just this deduction of the Greek god-names from Egypt as merely his own opinion, which all the less can be |364| decisive because he lacked the essential means of judgment and the records which are available to us (94). What an entirely different world would have dawned for the still-alert father of history had he known the old Hebrew records, (and known) that the first Bacchic orgies of Greece came from those Phoenicians who settled in Boeotia with the Tyrian Cadmus. Concerning the mysteries of Samothrace, he expressed the decided opinion that the island had received them from the Pelasgians, who first lived there before dwelling among the Athenians.

A peculiar narrative of the Ionian historian is the sole, yet only apparent, reason which can motivate a few researchers to seek the first source of the Cabiri cult in *Egypt*. At Memphis Cambyses had gone into the temple of Hephaestos and had greatly ridiculed the image. For it was the likeness of a pygmy, similar to the Phoenician *Pataikoi*. The blasphemer had even forced his way into the sanctuary of the Cabiri, in which none but the priest had been allowed to go, and with great levity burned the images, for they also resembled the images of Hephaestos. However, the comparison of the images of Hephaestos and of the Cabiri with those of the Phoenician tutelary gods would just as readily permit the opposite derivation of the Egyptian Cabiri from the dwarf gods of Phoenicia since, according to testimonies just as irrefutable, this land belonged to the oldest locales of the Cabiri. Therefore nothing concerning the initial arrival of the Cabiri cult may be concluded from that history. Even stranger in itself is the report that the Cabiri have been seen in Memphis in pygmy form. We do not wish to say how this form tallies with that representation according to which Hephaestos is the highest god of the Cabiri system as well as of the Egyptian system, and all other gods only emanations from him. How does such a picture even agree with the very names of the great gods, which are so generally ascribed to the Cabiri? One of the earlier investigators wanted to clear away the difficulty through exegesis, something impossible because there are indubitable evidences that the same gods |365| were depicted in dwarf style also outside of Egypt. In pictorial representations, likewise according to the poets, the old man Anchises bears the native Penates in his hand from Troy, a proof at least of the smallness of these images representing the deities which were related directly to the Cabiri. One could be tempted to say: the first Cabiri at least were all serving deities and accordingly were depicted as boys, as was the Etruscan-Roman Camillus. But boys are not dwarfs. More appropriate is the following account, especially since it rests on a representation which demonstrably was extant. As gods and as the most ancient of beings, they would necessarily be conceived in venerable form and as old persons; [but as serving beings or] as Camillus, youthful and as boys. The crude yet candid idol-sculpture only knew how to unite these conflicting concepts in the form of dwarfs. Indeed a fact should be admitted which also is justifiable on other grounds, namely that only the first Cabiri were depicted in such form; for the Cabiri at Memphis were seen in pygmy form only as sons of Hephaestos, only so far as themselves Hephaestian (*Hephäste*). Moreover we believe there is found therein a feature otherwise familiar to the human power of imagination, and again reminiscent of Old German and Norse representations, namely conceiving of great powers, more magical than natural, as associated with the dwarf form. By virtue of an old derivation, anything but plainly objectionable, our German word *"Zwerg"* [in Old German *"Tuwerg"*] has the Greek *"Theurgos"* as root, and hence from its origin has the meaning of "a being of magical power." [Who doesn't remember the artful, as it were "Hephaestian," dwarfs of Norse heroic sagas?] We may even recall our little gnomes, of which our gallant countryman Georg Agricola, so true-hearted, used to tell; for even they are, so to speak, sons of Hephaestos who have dealings with metals and even construct weapons from them (104). Since therefore the concept of supernatural strength is connected directly with the form of pygmies, it couldn't be surprising when those who are thought of as dwarfs, in a new twist |366| be conceived as giants; not astonishing when Hercules is named among the Idaean Dactyli[7](who were) conceived as still smaller, and when that shapeless image of the most ancient Cabiri [later] transfigured itself into the splendid forms of the Dioscuri (107).

Therefore even the report on their form leads back to the concept of magical, theurgic powers. Finally, the meaning which is expressed through their common name might deserve investigation. About this there is virtually one opinion among all researchers. According to the meaning of a similar-sounding Hebrew word, the name "Cabiri" expresses the concept of mighty, powerful gods. All other scruples against this interpretation (108) are practically overwhelmed by the single consideration that precisely these gods always and everywhere, together and singly, were called "the great," "the mighty." But what guarantee is there that the word "Cabiri" expressed just this concept? Not without reason there still remains the doubt that only the higher gods of the Cabiri system actually were called "the great." Moreover the name sounds too general, not sufficiently precise for the distinctive concept to allow us to be enticed by the initial resemblance. The inquiry of itself presses us once again to comprehend the characteristics of the Cabiri together in one image. The first Cabiri were magical or, to speak more precisely, theurgic, those powers or natures bringing the higher gods to realization. Yet not singly, but only in their insoluble sequence and chain do they practice the magic by which the transcendent is drawn into reality. The gods brought to revelation through them henceforth stand with them again in a magical connection. The whole Cabiri-series thus forms a magical chain binding the lowest with the highest. No link of this chain is permitted to be ineffectual or to withdraw, lest the magic pass away. Just as it is the appearance of both of the Dioscuri or only the sign of two paired lights which is a good omen to the seafarers, in the same way only in concert are the Cabiri the great salvation-bringing gods, and they are honored not singly, but only in common (112). |367| Therefore, if it was supposed to express completely their mutual nature, the name must have signified the concept of beings united insolubly (as the Dioscuri), and indeed united magically. Had one now to invent the name for the accepted concept, no more adequate one would be devised than that of "Cabiri," so long as one derives it [not, as is customary, from the Hebrew "*Kābbir*," which only means "*powerful*," and not even this with certainty, but] from another word of the same language, which embraces both the concept of an insoluble union and that of magic (113).

If then this explanation proves to be the more probable one, due to the exact coincidence of word and object, it is brought to a certainty by an additional similarity, unanticipated but therefore confirming it all the more. One finds among the ancient Etruscans an assembly of gods, a whole group of gods belonging together; their individual names were unknown, but all together they were called *Consentes* and *Complices,* which is merely an elucidation, indeed a literal translation, of the name "Cabiri" insofar as it has the meaning we have ascribed to it. They consisted of six male and six female beings, but in addition to them there was Jupiter, to whom they collectively were subordinate. If one considers the sexual duality of all ancient deities, not just that in one and the same nature both sexes were united artificially, but rather that each personality or, so to speak, each gradation in the progression of gods was designated by both a male and female deity; then here again is revealed that Cabiri number seven, resolving itself in Jupiter as unity (117). Different gods, they were yet all together as one (118). As is known historically, the Pelasgian colonists had brought their gods there from Teucris; to Lavinia's coast Aeneas exported the Trojan Penates, [which are one with the Cabiri natures]. And Varro attests that just these deities of Teucris were called *Complices* because only in concert could they live and die. It would be impossible to add anything to this expression or to indicate in a finer way the genuine idea of these associated gods. And so |368| again the meaning of the name discovered by research is authentic for the inner significance of the Cabiri system, a testimony for our interpretation developed initially from the sequence of these gods. The holy, revered teaching of the Cabiri, in its profoundest significance, was the representation of insoluble life itself as it progresses in a sequence of levels from the lowest to the highest, a representation of the universal magic and of the theurgy ever abiding in the whole universe, through which the invisible, indeed the super-actual, incessantly is brought to revelation and actuality. It is true that it was scarcely expressed in these terms there in Samothrace; the initiation into the mysteries had more the intention of binding one to the higher gods for life and death than of passing on information regarding the universe. The lower deities were viewed as theurgic means of this binding, and as such also were revered. This magic did not extend downwards into the visible world, but upwards. Through the consecrations received, the initiate himself became a link of that magical chain, himself a Kabir, taken up into the unbreakable relation and *joined* to the army of the higher gods, as the old inscription expresses it. In *this* sense the Cabiri or their servants might well be called inventors of magical singing, as Socrates says the child in us must continually be exorcised and must be healed as with magical singing until it is free of the fear of death (120). On the one hand directing itself wholly toward feeling and life, on the other hand the actual teaching may be conveyed quite clearly, likely because the chorus of the gods was depicted by the round dance of the stars. And what nobler symbol of the basic idea can be found than the insolubly linked movement of these heavenly lights, in which choir no element can be lacking without the whole crashing together; of which the truest statement would be that only together were they born, and only together can they die! In the course of time many things may be covered over (though we be unaware of it), much may be darkened and divested of significance (a fate of many nobler and better teachings). But whatever |369| concealment it may have endured, whatever turns it may have taken, the basic idea remains indestructible, the whole of the original doctrine unmistakable, a belief rescued from remote primitive times which, of all paganism, is the purest and closest to the truth.

The attempt to decipher a belief of the distant past seems not wholly unworthy for the celebration of this day. For research into the past occupies the greatest part of all scientific endeavor. Whether it is the most ancient characteristics, military exploits and writings of the people which are researched, whether the image of ruined creations of a rich nature be restored from almost unrecognizable copies, whether the traces be sought of the ways which the earth followed in its development: these investigations always proceed to times past. Of all worthy objects of study, however, the worthiest remains that which once united people inwardly, in which thousands, some of the best of their age, came to know the highest dedication of life. In the later period of the Roman empire the once holy name of the Cabiri was profaned through flattery; on coins not only the bust of the pious Antoninus or of Marcus Aurelius appeared, but even the head of a Domitian along with the inscription of the Cabiri deities. To us the finest employment of the name would be granted in that moment when it also recalls that Cabiri-like alliance, through which the power of a truly Typhonian realm was first broken,[8] and at last its final convulsions stifled, one which threatened to end only in general demoralization. But every more unusual expression, every more artistic turn of phrase, expresses the simple affection itself with which we rejoice in our all-beloved king, and in which, as in the ardent vow for his long-lasting welfare, we are in accord with all His people.

(The Postscript is not a part of the text proper, but follows it on an unnumbered page in the Schröter edition. It appears as page 423 in the edition by Schelling's son.)

Postscript

According to its original designation the preceding treatise belongs to a series of works which relate to *Die Weltalter* as common focus. That it appears sooner due to external circumstances cannot alter that designation, and in the wider circle in which it will be distributed in the book trade it will thus appear as a supplement to that work. This circumstance does not nullify its independence, since hopefully it will be granted that it can also stand entirely by itself, without any such relation. Not in itself but only in the intention of the author a supplement to another work, it is at once a beginning and a transition to some others the intention of which is to bring the actual primordial system of humanity to light from long eclipse, according to scientific development and where possible in an historical manner. For the knowledge attained up to a certain point is inseparable from history, and the transition from the one to the other is practically necessary. Not by chance do the particulars of the Samothracian system precede the more general inquiry; it was intentional to lay this at the foundation; for the Cabiri doctrine is as a key to all the rest, through its great antiquity as well as through the clarity and simplicity of its outlines. So much therefore concerning the broader context of this treatise, which after all must be taken entirely on its own, and also will be evaluated entirely on its own, according to its specific contents.

2. Schelling's Notes

⟨Introductory Statement⟩

Everyone who is no stranger to investigations of this kind will readily believe, without needing to be convinced, that it would have been easier and more agreeable had the author incorporated the material of the following notes into the text itself instead of as presently separating it out. However etymological research and the like, which concerns the comparision of passages and words of ancient writers, is not suitable for a public lecture, especially before a diverse audience. Therefore the author had to be resigned to the disadvantages arising from the separation. Above all the disadvantage that many a contention has been made outright which could find easier acceptance if introduced gradually and developed step by step from the individual analyses to which I have referred here. Therefore, because the notes exceed the text in length, it seemed well in the circumstances to make them wholly independent of it. In reference to such matters I therefore remark that much must be introduced which serves as support, not for the isolated interpretations but for the entire system of interpretation which has been presented here for the first time. A few points must thus appear to go beyond the text which are actually needed to undergird it. Therefore whoever wants to judge the aspect of the whole will all the less be able to avoid devoting serious study to the notes. If it should appear that almost too scrupulous diligence is given to the linguistic discussions, still it is more agreeable to the author to be rebuked for this reason rather than to be praised for the contrary. For such inquiries are nothing at all if not pursued with strictness and frequently painstaking care.

4) At that time when large tracts of Asia would have been covered continuously, others for a time, the lowlands of Samothrace also were inundated, as the inhabitants reported; on the highest mountain peaks they had sought aid with persistent vows to the native gods. Diodorus Siculus (5.47) adds that around the circumference of the whole island still stand altars which identify the limits of the peril then and the deliverance.

7) Iliad 13. 10 - 14.

21) Scholia ⟨Parisina ⟩ to Apollonius Rhodius *Argonautica* 1. 917.

29) The uncertainty of etymological explanations, particularly of the names of gods, derives above all from the fact that each deity is capable (of possessing) very many and very different attributes. It would be remarkable if the etymology did not succeed in extracting some one meaning of each name which agreed with some one attribute of the deity. Therefore above all else it is necessary for the researcher to know the basic concept of a deity, the root as it were of all its attributes; otherwise perhaps a multitude of derivations will stream in upon him with no one of them carrying with it firm conviction, while he passes over the true one even as almost of itself it presents itself to him, because he lacks a conception of the meaning resulting from it. But these

fundamental concepts are only determined through the position which each deity occupies in the general system of the gods. Therefore whoever fails to recognize at least its basic features would only conjecture and experiment haphazardly, but without arriving at any certainty or avoiding numerous blunders. So when Bochart explains the name Axieros from the Hebrew *'hzy 'rṣ,** *Achsi-Eres,* (the latter transliteration is Schelling's) *"the earth is mine,"* this is surely simply enough, but in principle we are no more advanced by that than the Greek, when he sought in his *Demeter* a *Gemeter* or "earth-mother." Indeed Ceres is also Mother Earth, but this is a derivative concept, not the original one. But if one be completely satisfied with general conceptions such as *magnipotens, perfecte sapiens* and the like, where is then a certainty in interpretation, where a trace of the precision and rigor which we encounter in all the concepts of antiquity? It is self-evident that one should know the language in which etymologies are drawn, not just from dictionaries, but from the sources and from its first roots. But even that does not suffice, without the still more refined knowledge of what the grammarians call the *proprietas verborum;* for many a word can have an entirely accidental meaning, or otherwise not belong in that special context to which they ascribe it in the contemporary interpretation. It would be useful, even necessary, for the etymological interpreter of the names of the gods to pay attention to the analogy with proper nouns in the same language from which the interpretation is made. The expert may judge to what extent I myself satisfy these principles and requirements now in the following attempt at interpretation.

31) (Schelling presents an extended argument linking the Hebrew roots *yrš** — "take possession of, inherit," and *rwš** or *ryš** — "be in want, poor.") . . . the concept of lack, of hunger, is the first, after which follows next that of drawing to oneself, seizure, occupancy. Written in Hebrew the name would be *ᵓahᵃšiērôš,*[9] which reads literally as *Achsieros,* following the soft pronunciation always observed in the transference of proper nouns. And so it would in the end be the name *Achas-Weros* itself, only according to another dialect. . . . (After discussing Persian roots, he links the name with that of the Persian king, Ahasuerus.) But how? A masculine king's name from a female deity! Why not? Chiefly because of the sexual ambiguity of all deities, the female deities may also be thought of as masculine. . . .

32) . . . The fact that in the explanation given of *Axieros* we pass from the concept of hunger immediately to that of (wistful) longing (*schmachtenden Sehnsucht*) cannot surprise one who knows that our presently more refined German *"Schmacht"* originally (as still in Low German and in a few compounds) was wholly synonymous with "hunger," and *"Schmacht"* (an ancient word) is hunger. . . .

44) Damascius, *De primis principiis: "Sidonioi de kata ton auton sungraphea (Eudemon) pro pantōn Chronon hupotithentai, kai POTHON kai Homichlēn."* ("The Sidonians posit Time before all else, and Desire and

Fog.") Here *time* obviously has the same significance as *Zeruane akherene*, the limitless time in the Parsee system. Because the gods come forth in a succession, they themselves are only offspring of the almighty time. According to a remarkable fragment, likewise from Damascius' *De primis principiis,* this limitless time was regarded as in itself the indifferent (neutral), which just for that reason is all; although as such is to be grasped only with reason ⟨*Verstand*⟩, only in thought. . . . But this same time in its operation is the establisher of all difference or, as it is expressed in an original Persian text ⟨*Zend-Avesta*⟩: "The true creator is *time,* which knows no limits, has nothing over it, has no root, and both has been and will be eternal." . . . In our language therefore we would say: "According to the old Parsee doctrine, limitless time is that in which unity and difference are themselves established as One." . . . Everyone who understands the concept has held that this limitless time is no *summus Deus.* . . . It cannot itself be designated a *principium superius,* for it permeates everything. But it is also not the mere eternity which is referred to in current "school concepts" . . . .

45) Eusebius, *Praeparatio evangelica* 2.10 *ineunt.* To translate *sunkrasis* by "mixture" ⟨*Mischung*⟩ readily evokes a false conception. I translated it as "contraction" ⟨*Zusammenziehung*⟩ in the sense in which two vowels are elided. Even "coalescence" ⟨*Verschmelzung*⟩ would be acceptable; in general the word designates a binding in which the one is moderated by the other, a *temperamentum.* . . .

47) . . . ⟨Schelling criticizes the equations of Sainte-Croix (Phaethon = Axieros, Venus = Axiokersa, Pothos = Cadmillus) and of Creuzer (Pothos = Eros).⟩ But according to linguistic usage *Pothos* very definitely differs from *Eros.* . . . *Pothos* is longing for a lost or now absent good. As *Pothos* relates to the past, so does *Himeros* to the contemporary, the present . . . *Eros* is the initial kindling, the desire which precedes possession, therefore strives toward the yet future . . . Therefore among the Samothracian deities the concept of *Pothos* fits only Ceres, for she alone pines or longs for one who is lost. . . . According to ancient teaching, every longing indicates to some extent a nature, even this initial and primordial instance, in a prior condition of unity with that for which it longs. . . . Even that first nature has been placed by means of a prior separation in that condition of loneliness, therefore of lack, of need, in which it appears as longing. But no less so in artistic conception was *Pothos* distinguished from *Eros.* . . .

49) . . . According to Euripedes, *Phoenissae* 689, Ceres and Proserpina are called the *diōnumoi theai.*

52) Creuzer III, 455ff. and 533ff.; IV, 247; et al.

58) *Haides kai Dionysos ho autos.* Plutarch, *De Iside et Osiride* 28.

59) Plutarch, *De Iside et Osiride* 78: *archei* (Herodotus 2.123: *archegeteuei) kai basileuei tōn tethnēkotōn.*

64) It is obvious that our view is the latter. Axiokersa and Axiokersos together construct the cosmos through a twofold magic, for the later one does

not counteract or cancel out the earlier, but rather subdues it. This would be the case even if the name merely expressed the general concept of the magician. Yet it is surmised that the original was not *Kersos,* but *Kersor.* . . . Then that *Chores-Ur, Chrysor,* or *Kersor* would be equivalent in name to *Oser-Es,* or *Osiris.* . . .(In a very protracted argument, Schelling links *Kersor* and *Osiris* with the Hebrew root *ḥrš,** which appears in a word meaning "to fabricate," and in another word meaning "magic art." He also links both with fire, and argues on the basis of evidence from inscriptions that *Kersor-Osiris* is a fire-conjurer — *Feuerbeschwörer,* one who moderates fire — *Feuerbesänftiger,* and an initiator — *Eröffner* of nature. Quoting Heraclitus, he says:) "The world is an eternal living fire, which at intervals . . . flares up and is extinguished." Thus there is one power which ignites it (that is Ceres, Isis, Persephone,or whatever one otherwise calls the first nature); another which banks it . . ., moderates it and thereby becomes the first initiator of nature, opening it up into mild life and gentle corporeality. This latter power is Osiris or Dionysos. . . .

67) . . . Creuzer must on the whole agree with this because for him Axieros is the highest deity. Nevertheless in II, 297ff. he seeks other connections, the purpose of which almost seems to be the creation for Kadmilos of a different significance than that of Hermes (cf. p. 317), which surely would have to be the case if he were to be the subordinate to the other three.

71) Entirely unnecessary is Bochart's explanation (of "Kadmiel"), *Geographiae sacrae,* Pt. 1, from *dwm** and the meaning *ministrare* derived from Arabic. *Kadmilos* is quite simply *ḳadimîʾēl** from *ḳdmy,** *prior, antecedens.* The name "Kadmiel," so written, appears in the *later* books of the Old Testament and indeed as the name of a priest, a Levite. Cf. Ezra 2:40, 3:9, Nehemiah 7:43, et al. Certainly it doesn't mean, as is customarily explained, . . . *quem Deus beneficiis praevenit,* but rather one who "stands before God" . . . or one who "is herald, messenger, proclaimer of God" . . . or "who sees the countenance of God" . . . .

72) The *mlʾk hpnym,** Isaiah 63:9, also plainly *mlʾk yhwh** in Exodus 23:20ff. A detailed explanation of this concept is found in the first part of *The Ages of the World,* VIII, 272ff. (IV, 648ff.). . . . What the angel of the presence is in the Old Testament, what Kadmilos is in the Greek mysteries, what Hermes-Camillus is in Etruscan religion, so is *Metatron* in the later Jewish philosophy. . . . He is the highest-ranking angel and accordingly elevated above all angels, i.e., all natures which are only messengers or instruments of the highest deity, just as in our view Kadmilos is elevated above the first Cabiri. . . .

74)Creuzer interprets it this way, *Symbolik* . . . II, 333. In this generally excellent work it does not seem advantageous that the theory of emanation is made the basis of all explanations, owing to a very definite philosophical outlook which one finds developed at the end of the fourth part and which is only with violence forced upon Christianity as upon antiquity. While this viewpoint, as something entirely foreign, can be separated from this work the invaluable benefit of which is, by means of nobler ideas in union with comprehensive scholarship, to have broken the path for a profounder knowledge of the whole of mythology, it (the viewpoint) yet remains unchallenged throughout. I expecially think it correct to mention here something which actually should have been noted previously, that by the light in which he places the doctrine of Ceres and Proserpina Creuzer has provided the initial way to the view which has developed in the present discussion. He has shown incontrovertibly, especially in IV, par. 39, that Ceres is the first of the natures, and the foundation on which this (i. e., Schelling's)systematic interpretation rests is the correct understanding of this thesis, namely that the first nature is not taken to be the highest, as does Creuzer, but rather as lying at the basis of all. When however this very same gifted scholar yields to Zoëga in the interpretation of the Samothracian mysteries, and with him regards Axieros as the highest deity of the Egyptian system, this position conflicts with the analogy of the mythological principles he himself erected elsewhere.

75) Therefore also the restriction elsewhere (by Creuzer). "This procession from the One nature and return into it was doubtless presented to the *educated* as fundamental doctrine, which indeed the *crude Pelasgian* was not in a position to grasp. Instead one presented him with a series of astral gods and meteorites associated with them, idols infused with astral power and magically efficacious, etc."

80) But Dionysos is also a demiurge and indeed, so to speak, the demiurge overcoming Hephaestos who releases the creation from the bonds of necessity and sets it forth in free multiplicity. This apparent contradiction is resolved through the general observation that a nature (*Wesen*) or principle which stands higher than another and to that extent is its contrast (prevailing over it), nevertheless can with that one belong to one class over against a still higher (principle). What follows is for those who can understand a whole from mere indications! Zeus is also again Dionysos, as now and then has already been expressly shown (see the quotations in Creuzer, III, 397 compared with 416). That is, Zeus is again related to the first three potencies, as the second is related to the first. I say to the first three, although we previously enumerated four. For when viewed more profoundly, Ceres is no arithmetical number. According to Pythagorean doctrine she is the mother of numbers, the intelligible dyad with which the monad engenders all actual numbers. Persephone is the first number (*protogonos*), the arithmetical "One." Thus Zeus is again related to 1,2,3, as 2 is related to 1, and reciprocally 2 is related to 1 not otherwise than 4 is related to 1,2,3. The number of Zeus is always the fourth number. But moreover, Dionysos returns once again to the higher potency. Axiokersos is Dionysos in the lowest potency.

84) Strangely enough the historian Mnaseas breaks off with Dionysos, whether because he himself received no higher initiation, or whether, more probably the case, because sacred awe restrained him from uttering the final

secret. The scholiast says that *a few* add a fourth. Therefore not all reached this number (of Kadmilos) with which the meaning of the whole first opened up. No author carried the series beyond this number. Zeus, Venus, Apollo, and others were named singly only outside the series. All the more natural is it to continue the thread, broken off with Kadmilos in the case of the ancient scholiast, by means of other fragments which occur among the remains of Phoenician cosmogonies. . . . Therefore Sanchuniathon, after speaking of the Corybants and Cabiri, proceeds: "*To time itself* (*Zur Zeit derselben*) was born a certain Eljun with the name 'the highest'." Through a simple alteration the meaning would be brought out: "*After them*" (*Nach denselben*). But for our purpose it is unnecessary, all the more because one concedes for this fragment, if no higher origin, still that its root can be assigned to the myth of the birth of Zeus, watched over (so remarkably!) by the Curetes and Corybants. The actual name of the highest god of Genesis 14:18, whose priest is that Malki-Sedek, wonderfully emerging from the darkness of the primordial time, is Eljun, the name of the god who possesses "heaven and earth" (indeed the Cabiri duality was also so expressed), therefore of the lord of the world, the demiurge. If one may here make use of the valid observation made very well by Creuzer, that the priest represented the god and indeed also bore his name, therefore Malki-Sedek is the name of the highest god himself. Wherefore he also says that indeed the most ancient Jewish writings which in this respect followed certain traditions, for example the book Sohar, the Sepher Jetzira, and the Beresit Rabba (cf. Bochart, *Geographiae sacrae,* p. 707) express the name of Zeus by *ṣdḳ,** "Sedek." But everyone conversant with linguistic usage knows that Malki-Sedek means nothing other than "the perfect (*vollkommen*) king, the final (*vollendet*) ruler," therefore precisely that one whom I Timothy 6:15 calls: *ho makarios* (even this in the sense of "final") *kai monos dunastēs, ho basileus tōn basileuontōn kai kurios tōn kurieuontōn.* The other natures, next to him most perfect, indeed rule, but they rule only as instruments, in the manner of servants of an earthly king, not as autocrats but as deputies. This all leads to the following. The seven sons of Sydyk, ("Sadik," according to Damascius ⟨*Vita Isidori* 302⟩) are authentically called "the Cabiri," Eusebius, *Praeparatio evangelica* 1.10. Here the meaning is the same as when the first (lowest) Cabiri are called sons of Hephaestos. That is, they all together are only Sydyk, who, a final ruler, lives only in them; they are merely like the single parts of a whole, the powers making the father actual and perceptible who in that respect also precede him in revelation or perceptibility. Thus whoever wanted to conclude from this relationship something for the representation of emanation, would err. . . . Therefore the Cabiri are sons of Sydyk and that king of Salem was priest of the same Sydyk (Sedek). Thus perhaps it would be permissable to say that this Malki-Sedek was the first known Cabir (indeed even the priests and initiates are so called), to whom the system up to the fourth number was disclosed which in the course of ages was to be revealed in complete clarity up to the seventh, indeed the eighth, number.

Yet these most ancient links may be indicated only hesitantly. For it to be demonstrated by the most cautious researcher wholly from the sources, it is obvious that those evidences are still too inconclusive to base a proper assertion on them. However, a larger investigation, wider in scope and conducted from other aspects, could enhance its strength.

87) Liberality with explanations having recourse to deception, priestly trickery and like is certainly characteristic of the later time. Powers are credited to falsehoods which one scarcely ascribes to the truth. But antiquity was not so idiotic, even if it did not with deliberate cunning immediately suspect deception everywhere. Had there not resided in paganism something very earnest and more substantial than one thinks, how could monotheism have required so long a time to become its master? . . .

88) *Oida ego kai Platona prosmarturounta Herakleitoi, graphonti. Hen to sophon, mounon legesthai ouk ethelei, kai ethelei Zenos onoma.* (Clement of Alexandria, *Stromata* 5.115.1) The monotheism which acknowledges in the name of god only one *personality* or one wholly simple power may well be called "Mohammedan." No proof is needed that it is not from the New Testament. That it is also not from the Old Testament, see *The Ages of the World,* part one ⟨VIII⟩ [272ff.].

90) I say: "a scientific system," not a merely instinctive knowing as in visions or in clairvoyance or in other similar arts which one contrives these days, wherein a few renounce science directly and others wish where possible to introduce a knowing without science. Because the text does not maintain, but only sets forth as a possibility, the existence of such a primordial system older than all written documents, which is the common source of all religious doctrines and representations; accordingly I freely concede that whoever believes it does not have to be recognized as the most probable ⟨hypothesis⟩, may object to this allegation of future research seeking to establish it (the primordial system) in its entirety rather than in one aspect, and in light of this declaration may proclaim himself opposed to the hypothesis.

94) Besides it cannot literally be accepted that the *names* of most gods had come to Greece from Egypt. Perhaps if Herodotus' knowledge had been more extensive, far from deriving the names of Greek gods from Egypt he would have doubted whether the Egyptian names themselves are of Egyptian origin. . . . The doubt which has been expressed in regard to the Egyptian gods' names may in time also be heard in regard to the Indian ⟨names⟩; the very great significance of this is obvious. That a people does not dare to change the names of gods which it has not itself invented is far more probable than the contrary. A magic power was also joined to the names, and what the general superstition held regarding incantations, namely that they worked only in the language in which they were handed down, applied as well to names of gods. So up to the time of Diodorus Siculus, along with the ancient cult Samothrace retained in sacred use not only the ancient names but also certain expressions of a characteristically ancient speech . . .

104) (Schelling concludes a discussion of mountain-dwelling dwarfs in German literature and popular culture by equating one of the common terms for such beings, "*Kobold*," with the Greek *kobalos*.) . . . Due to the countless instances of the interchangeability of *R* and *L*, there is no doubt that *kobaloi* is equivalent to *kobaroi;* and that this has the same *Etymon* as *kabeiros* is just as little in doubt. Thereby the connection proven in the representations is also exhibited in the names. . . .

107) . . . If one doesn't wish to believe in absurd Jewish fables, one can interpret *bny h³lhym** only by "worshippers of the true god," who were depicted as though cut off from other humans and as a distinctive race. Thus they were the initiates, so to speak, of the first and oldest of the mysteries; what was supposed to expand gradually, as from a central point, was from the beginning somewhat secluded, entrusted only to a part of the human race. Is it not striking that all higher and finer belief originally comes forth both in Greece and elsewhere under the form of secret teachings? Transitory and local causes (for this) may not always and everywhere be supposed; instead the mystery, the seclusion, appears given just as originally and from the beginning, simultaneously with the thing itself. All possessors of the most ancient mysteries became *sons* of the highest god, as were the Dios-Kuri who in their origin manifestly were human twins, and who finally passed over among the Cabiri. From these higher natures descended the first human heroes, the Nephilim (*Niflungen*?) who were mighty so long as they lived and were still great and renowned in the underworld (*Niffelheim* of the Old Norse mythology?), cf. Isaiah 14:9. Everyone may seek to correlate further these wonderous intimations as well as he can, but it is very natural to look back to the oldest times for an explanation of such a universal mystery-form. What was the strict exclusiveness of the Jewish people but an arrangement similar to the mysteries, only that it drew a dividing wall not between persons from the same group, but between a people and all others. Christianity was the first to cancel all barriers.

108) Namely from the Hebrew *kabîr,** "mighty, powerful." There are a great number favoring this interpretation. . . . The principal reservation against this interpretation is that the unqualified meaning of "mighty" is not demonstrable, at least not without calling upon the Arabic for support. Generally it seems to indicate only the concept of something mighty and powerful through a superabundance. . . .

112) On account of this proven fundamental concept (of their nature as inseparable) no use was made of the presumed discovery of different epochs in the history of the Samothracian cult. (There follows a critique of the views of Sainte-Croix, who thinks there were originally only two Cabiri, Heaven and Earth, the others being subsequent foreign additions to the system). This atomistic proceeding of interpreting through patchwork something which appears incomprehensible as a whole, should at least support itself with solid arguments. . . . Thus Varro not once says that the oldest form of the doctrine

was of two in number (Creuzer II, 291 note), but only that there were two *principes Dei.* Granted that it was actually his intention philosophically to trace all deities back to a duality lying at their foundation; still there is a clear distinction between "*two first*" deities lying at the basis of all, and "*two first*" in the sense of "*taken alone.*". . . it follows that he (Varro) conceived the series as continuous and not once in his philosophy stood still at the number two. On the other hand this progression could not prevent him from again tracing all (the whole series) back dualistically to a basic opposition of male and female. For all philosophy is led to such a duality lying at the basis of all, without thereby maintaining that there are only two *beings* (*Wesen*). . . .Here Varro decisively maintains a triad, not a duo, in the Samothracian representations. There is no doubt that the whole series unfolds from the three given basic concepts, or contrariwise, the whole sequence of numbers is restored to the triad. . . . That is to say, all the Cabiri natures are only continuous gradations, so that the same number or personality returns in different potencies, and all numbers revert to certain fundamental numbers, indisputably three . . . and the unbiased researcher will readily acknowledge that Varro's explanation is no small confirmation for the whole of our position. That triad lying at the basis of all can reduplicate itself progressively, and just as the three could be Persephone, Dionysos and Kadmilos, so they could also be Juno, Jupiter and Minerva, as Varro renders them in the passage just cited. . . .

113) (The Hebrew root is *hbr*,* which means "unite" or "be joined." Schelling finds reference in the Kabbala to the "associates" or "*Chabbirim*" of Metatron, whom he equates with Kadmilos. After expressing the wish for some researcher to go through the entire *Zohar,* he continues:) It is well-nigh sad to see how these inquiries into the true sources also have so completely gone astray. The key to ancient religions had been sought in Egypt's own obscure and indecipherable hieroglyphics. Now the talk is of nothing but India's language and wisdom. But the Hebrew language and writings, foremost the Old Testament, in which the roots of doctrine and the language itself of all ancient religious systems are clearly recognizable down to the details, lie unstudied. It is very desirable that these most venerable records soon pass from the hands of the mere theologian, into those of the purely historical researcher; as it is hoped that they be given an unbiased assessment and valued as sources at least as much as the Homeric poems and the narratives of Herodotus. This is not to say that the purely historical researcher and the theologian cannot be united in one person. In this case all must finally concur. But first, although it is beginning to be generally understood, it will be difficult to hold that interpreting dogma with authority from within and with authority from without makes no difference in the true evaluation. It is only that the latter case, as in all merely negative undertakings, more often leads to intolerance and shallowness than does the former, which at least is a positive, uniting effort, seeking coherence. The name "Cabir," or actually *Chabir*, is an Old Testament term which expresses simultaneously inseparable connection

and magical union. . . . It would be a quite natural expectation also to find traces of the name "Cabir" in other Oriental languages. . . . (Schelling notes connections with a pre-Zoroastrian Persian term; parallels with Indian terms are inconclusive.)

117) Hereby Jupiter must be conceived in a double relation: once, insofar as he himself is one of the seven; then insofar as he is Zeus the beginning, Zeus the middle, and Zeus the end, as the Orphics say.

118) Therefore (one) in basis, if one removes in thought the requisite separation, just as "Elohim" in the plural is by the verb united into the singular. (Compare *The Ages of the World,* VIII, 273, (IV, 649) - - footnote by the editor.)

120) *Phaedo* 77E.

3. Letters from Schelling

(These translated excerpts from letters are taken from G. L. Plitt, editor, *Aus Schellings Leben, In Briefen,* Vol. II (Leipzig: Verlag von S. Hirzel, 1870), pp. 359 - 65, 445 - 46. Several other letters which refer to *The Deities of Samothrace* have been omitted because they say nothing significant about it. These letters show that Schelling promptly circulated his manuscript to selected persons, and indicate something of his relation to Creuzer.)

Schelling to Georgii

October 13, 1815

. . . The occasion for the present lines is provided by a just published treatise which I believe it obligatory to forward to you, indeed with the hazard that you will regard such a thing not worth reading. To be sure, it is full of much vain erudition as such treatises universally are; but you would not for that reason fail to recognize its actual intention, especially if you happen to read the notes and what I said therein about our Old Testament books. All this which I carry on and, not merely for my sake but also on account of the matter, *must* be carried on, nevertheless leads back to the one great goal, which alone occupies me as you and to which, thank God, I draw gradually closer. I feel deeply at this moment the death of the noble Rieger[10] whose passing was a great loss to many people (and for whose fine biography I have not yet thanked you), because much in this treatise would directly appeal to him as a competent scriptural scholar and exegete. For few are the actual, or rather so-called, scholars to whom my true intention will be comprehensible or, if comprehensible, then agreeable. . . .

Schelling to Silvestre de Sacy[11]

October 15, 1815

. . . In fact the little book which I sent to *you* was also born from this scholarship, although the title seems to turn to another subject. Most learned sir, you are not unaware that there have been still others after Gerhard Vossius and Samuel Bochart who suspected that the names of the Cabiri deities, and also this collective noun itself, derived from the Phoenician language. I also have been of that opinion but for their explanations, which indeed seemed to me less justified, I have substituted others. If these be well-grounded, the affair is by no means of trifling moment for the whole knowledge of antiquity and especially for mythology, as *you* are well aware and this little book of mine amply shows. Therefore I would wish for you, most learned sir and the arbiter most expert of all in these matters, to observe and pronounce a judgment whether or not they have been demonstrated. I do not ask that you do this for myself, but for the sake of the issue itself. Nay, rather your class of that Institute, which bears its name from the study of antiquity, cannot think this alien to it. To be sure, in the reports of the celebrated Academy of Inscriptions, to which that of yours succeeded, it was Fréret who, first after those more ancient authors, began to treat the religion of the Cabiri (although I can scarcely endorse his treatment); and in the same journal there presently appeared the most renowned work of your colleague Sainte-Croix on the Mysteries of the Ancients, of which I too have made considerable use. These therefore are the reasons for my hope that you will not disdain to render an opinion on this matter. . . .

Schelling to Creuzer

Munich, October 15, 1815

The previous kindness, in no way deserved on my part, with which you honored me hitherto by sending your work (most recently on Plotinus), allows me, as it were, to address you as *friend*. Long have I wished through some means for a reciprocal gift — not to offset yours, but yet to express my gratitude with something more than mere words. External circumstances have pulled loose from me, perhaps yet too soon, one of the works out of the whole which for years has occupied me. The fact that in a principal point I contradict you, and in a few related points deviate from you, could not restrain me from sending this to you. For in part I am conscious at no time to have violated my inherent respect for you, and in part persuaded that you also would view that as a gain, in which I could be correct over against you, if I be correct. For it nevertheless leads on the whole to the goal toward which you wanted to direct this branch of scholarship. But well could I have avoided submitting to you, whose productions all bear the stamp of ultimate and most precise perfection, a little work the deficiency and, due to the remissness of the press, still heightened imperfection of which I am only too well aware. Nevertheless I hope to experience precisely from you the fairest reception and, in your approving or contradicting observations, in both cases instructive, to find ample substitutes for many insults which may threaten me from others in whose learned household my views are not deemed suitable. Often enough, while engaged in this as well as in the larger work, have I wished myself in your vicinity or you in mine. How much shorter then my way, from how many blunders could you have protected the unexperienced one! . . .

Schelling to Friedrich Schlegel[12]

Munich, January 10, 1816

. . . We all were complimented at seeing you here on the trip to Frankfurt. . . . Now I must anticipate whether a happy fate will bring us together again, or whether a more comprehensive scholarly task, with which I am occupying myself for several years, can perhaps become a means for us to meet again. May the accompanying little work in the meantime at least show you how I seek more and more in scholarly and historical inquiries to proceed from the general to the specific.

Schelling to Creuzer

Munich, October 11, 1820

I have still not thanked you, most honored sir and friend, for the precious gift of the second part of the new edition of your *Symbolik*. Being away to the end of August I received it rather late, scarcely was I till now in a position to cast a glance at this part, and I must now deny myself still longer the enjoyment of studying it. . . .

Lest this letter be filled wholly with personal matters, in reference to the fact that you, as I saw, have granted the honor of mentioning my etymology of the Cabiri-name, I wish to mention something I discovered long ago, that just this name actually appears in the book of Job — in my firm conviction ancient and pre-Mosaic — and indeed in a passage where the parallelism, so decisive in Hebrew poesie, with *Sons of Canaan* (Phoenicians) cannot be doubted. So that by *habîrîm** actually will be understood "Cabiri" (a people's name according to Suidas). Yet for the time being this is enough for you! . . . (The editor's (?) footnote to the next to last sentence reads:) Thus in the copied manuscript; intended is Job 40:30, where it reads *habārîm*.*

Notes to Part Two

[1]Aegina is an island in the Saronic Gulf, southwest of Athens. In 1811 important archaeological discoveries were made on Aegina, including notable sculptures. In 1812 Crown Prince Louis of Bavaria acquired the collection of art works, which was installed at the Glyptothek in Munich. In 1817 Johann Martin Wagner (1777-1858), a professor of art history, published a report on these art works from Aegina. Schelling wrote a series of notes on Wagner's report which were published together with it in the same volume. Schelling's notes are reprinted in his collected works as: *Kunstgeschichtliche Anmerkungen zu Johann Martin Wagners Bericht über die Aeginetischen Bildwerke*, 9, 111-206, (s3, 515-610).

[2]See section four of Part One for information about Zoëga and the other modern authors Schelling refers to by name in the materials translated here.

[3]The allusion is to Plato's *Symposium* 203B ff. At the banquet of the gods on the occasion of Aphrodite's birth, Poverty *(Penia)* united with Abundance or Resource (*Poros*) the son of Cunning (*Mētis*) as he lay in drunken sleep, and their offspring was Love (*Eros*).

[4]A note by an editor indicates that at this point there is a correction in the author's copy, which also contains the alternative reading: *"das sehnsüchtige Schmachten."*

[5]Actually Pothos means "longing," whereas Phaëton means "shining." Naphtali Lewis, *Samothrace*, . . . vol. 1, presents a critical text (no. 160) of Pliny's *Naturalis historia* 36.5.25, which reads: *"Is fecit Venerem et Pothon qui. . . ,"* with the variant *"Venerem et Pothon et Phaethontem."* Schelling reproduces this variant reading in his own footnote to this sentence. Evidently then Schelling himself, or more likely a typesetter, carelessly transposed in the text the names Pothos and Phaëton, thus accounting for the erroneous association of Phaëton with "longing."

[6]The Greek (of Clement of Alexandria, *Stromata* 5.115.1) which Schelling begins by paraphrasing, and then shifts into translating, as reproduced in his note 88 is in agreement with the text of Migne, *P. G.,* vol. 9, col. 172. Schelling's German translation of the quotation is: *"Das Eine weise Wesen will nicht das alleinige genannt seyn, den Namen Zeus will es!"* which I have rendered: "The One wise nature does not wish to be called that exclusively; it wishes the name 'Zeus'." Clearly the version of the *Ante-Nicene Fathers* (vol. 2, p. 471) will not do for this Greek: "The one thing that is wise alone will not be expressed, and means the name of Zeus." Whereas Schelling's translation is plausible, so is that of G. S. Kirk and J. E. Raven, *The Presocratic Philosophers* (Cambridge: Cambridge University Press, 1957): "One thing, the only truly wise, does not and does consent to be called by the name of Zeus" (No. 231, p. 204). Schelling's reading underlines the affirmative relation between the highest god and Zeus as a figure in the cult, in a way that the alternative reading does not. This is a good example of Schelling's practice of dealing scrupulously with original sources while at the same time picking that (plausible) interpretation which accords with his own views.

[7]The Idaean Dactyli were wizards and smiths whose origin is traced back to either or both of the two mountains called "Mt. Ida" (one in Crete and the other near Troy). Some of them practiced mysteries and initiatory rites and according to legend played a role in the formation of the Samothracian cult. Their numbers are variable, but one commonly stated total is ten (five males and five females), hence the appropriateness of the name (*"daktulos"* means "finger" in Greek). There is no general scholarly agreement on the exact nature of their close relation to the Curetes and Corybants (whom Schelling frequently mentions).

[8]Perhaps this is a reference to the recent defeat of Napoleon. Bavaria had been involved in the Napoleonic wars on the side of France and against Austria. But in late 1813, partially due to the influence of Crown Prince Louis, the Bavarian government altered its policy and joined the alliance which succeeded in defeating Napoleon in June of 1815.

[9]Schelling's text actually presents a Hebrew word which transliterates approximately as: ʾahᵃyēšîrôš. I have substituted ʾahᵃšîerôš, based on the conjecture that the printer transposed two

of the consonant-vowel combinations. The latter form is certainly closer to Schelling's own transliteration, so that I assume it is what he intended.

[10]This person is not readily identifiable. Perhaps intended is Karl Heinrich Rieger of Stuttgart (1726-1791), a theologian, preacher and biblical scholar, though Schelling could only have known him some 25 years before the date of this letter.

[11]This letter is written in Latin. Antoine-Isaac baron Silvestre de Sacy (1758-1838) was professor of Persian at the Collège de France and the principal founder in Europe of the disciplines of Arabic studies and Islamics. Schelling presented a memorial statement to the Bavarian Academy of Sciences (March 28, 1838) following his death. Cf. 10, 295-300 (s4, 469-74). The letter refers to the prestigious *Académie des inscriptions et belles-lettres* and to one of its periodicals, probably the *Mémoires de l'Academie* which began publication in 1717. Schelling mentions Nicolas Fréret (1688-1749) and Sainte-Croix. Fréret was a famous French antiquarian and secretary of the *Académie* who published his research in the *Mémoires*. Sainte-Croix was also a prominent member of the *Académie* (from 1777) as was de Sacy (from 1785). After being suspended during the French Revolution the *Académie* was reorganized in 1803. Schelling's mention of de Sacy's "class" refers either to the *Classe d'histoire et de littérature ancienne,* or to its subdivision, the *Section des langues anciennes.*

[12]Friedrich Schlegel (1772-1829) was the leader of the German Romantics and a friend of Schelling's since their youth.

Part Three

Philosophical Interpretation

Schelling's exposition of the Samothracian religion focuses on the Cabiri themselves. He interprets their natures and mutual relations as constitutive of a symbol system which depicts the divine in its ontological complexity and in its relation to worldly processes and human knowledge. The key statement summarizing his view bears repeating here.

> The holy, revered teaching of the Cabiri, in its profoundest significance, was the representation of insoluble life itself as it progresses in a sequence of levels from the lowest to the highest, a representation of the universal magic and of the theurgy ever abiding in the whole universe, through which the invisible, indeed the super-actual, incessantly is brought to revelation and actuality. (368)

The symbols derive from Samothrace itself, or from the larger context of Greek myth and religion which he uses to illumine the cult. But the underlying meaning which Schelling discovers in them (or reads into them), when expressed systematically, corresponds to his own ontology. To unlock the secrets of this "representation of insoluble life itself," as Schelling sees it and its implications, is the task in the following philosophical interpretation. First, I give a characterization of the conception of God and the consequent ontology which Schelling worked out in the six years prior to composing *The Deities of Samothrace*. Next I show in detail how the application of this system to the mysteries of Samothrace produces the ontologized mythology which Schelling believes to be a successful recreation of the "primordial system . . . which is the common source of all religious doctrines and representations." Finally, I look forward briefly to the vast philosophy of mythology and revelation which Schelling constructed in his later years, to show in what ways *The Deities of Samothrace* is a bridge to that enterprise.

1. The Conception of God in "The Ages of the World."

In 1809 there is evidence of a decisive shift in Schelling's thought. With the essay *Of Human Freedom* (1809) he began to work out a new conception of God derived in part from the bizarre writings of Jacob Boehme. Schelling recast Boehme's ideas in a much more sophisticated form, combined them with themes carried over from his own earlier works, and produced a unique speculative vision of the nature of God and of God's relation to the world. The *Stuttgart Lectures* (1810) built further upon the foundation laid by *Of Human Freedom,* and the project culminated in the vast and quite detailed philosophical theology of *The Ages of the World* (1811 - 1815)[1]

Ages is the watershed between what Schelling later called the "negative philosophy" and the "positive philosophy." Negative philosophy analyzes the dialectical structures of thought itself. It is purely rational philosophy concerned with a grasp of the conceptual structure, or the essence, of all things. Stated in Schelling's own terms, it is the reflection upon, and deduction of, the inherent relations of the "potencies" of being. As such, negative or rational philosophy is an a priori and speculative science. It moves exclusively within the realm of pure thought. It does not deal with (is incapable of dealing with) the fact of something's actual existence. Schelling's own negative philosophy culminates in the recognition that the power of freedom is required to transform the conceptual potencies into actual being. This means that the highest reality is not thought but will. The structures of thought and of the being which it comprehends are qualified by their ontological dependence on, and derivation from, will. The inadequacy of negative philosophy for the full understanding of actual (not just ideal) being is not recognized by other philosophers who stay within the framework of speculative idealism, and was not recognized by Schelling in his earlier phases prior to his preoccupation with will and the philosophy of freedom.

The positive philosophy succeeds where the negative philosophy had failed, for it develops a way to understand actually existing beings by reinstating reason and the potencies of being in their proper place as derivative from the exercise of will. However the changeover does not occur all at once. In a sense the demand for something like the positive philosophy is implicit in Schelling's writing as early as his *Philosophy and Religion* (1804),[2] in which he discussed the fall of the world of ideas away from the Absolute. This work signalled the decomposition of the "philosophy of identity," but he did not develop the analysis of free will until 1809. The works just prior to *Ages* lay the foundation for the advent of the positive philosophy, but its actual emergence begins midway in *Ages* itself.

The positive philosophy takes as its starting point the absolutely free will of God as the highest reality, and has as its goal the comprehension of actual being as produced by will. It consists of two stages. The first stage of the positive philosophy is the rational or deductive construction of the nature of being as the product of freedom. It consists of an account of the structure of God's being (which he wills for himself), and also of the "divine ideas" or the vision of a possible creation. It differs from the negative philosophy, which is also deductive in form, in that its speculative vision is one of being as subordinate to will. Yet the first stage of the positive philosophy cannot stand alone, for it is a merely speculative philosophy of the principles of actual being and requires validation by an examination of actual being itself. *Ages* contains both the elements of the negative philosophy (the conceptual potencies of being expressed in their most abstract form) and also the deductive part of the positive philosophy. *Ages* was to be continued to include as well the second stage of the positive philosophy: an empirical validation of the principles attained in the deductive or first stage. But Schelling saw that this was too vast a project to be continued within the limits of *Ages* itself and so broke off his work to pursue its implications elsewhere and more deliberately, leaving *Ages* itself unpublished, unfinished, and containing only a few hints of the course stage two was to take.

Schelling's God is one who freely creates a world in his own image. As is shown below in some detail, Schelling holds that the ontological structures of God and of the world parallel one another. This is because in creating God projects outside his own being a reduplication of the same powers and principles which constitute it. Furthermore, God in his self-revelation himself enters into the world he has created. His life in the world is seen in the mythologies and revelations in human history. Therefore the history of mythology and of religions should provide the corroboration of Schelling's philosophical theology, if he can only show that the portrait of the divine which is disclosed to human consciousness through mythology and historical religions is in agreement with those conceptual structures which he worked out in *Ages,* as a speculative philosopher of religion. In pursuit of this goal he eventually produced the lectures on mythology and revelation instead of continuing *Ages* itself. But the first step of the project of empirical confirmation was the exploratory essay, *The Deities of Samothrace.* The following exposition presents in outline the basic structure of God according to *Ages* and the works immediately preceding it, and then shows how Schelling interprets the Cabiri of Samothrace to conform to, or "verify" his philosophical concept of God.

In *Of Human Freedom* Schelling introduced the concept of a bipolar God, consisting of both a ground or center of power (non-being as *mē on),*[3] and God's actualized being. His position is neither monistic nor dualistic in any simple sense, but is rather a portrait of a God who constitutes himself as a duality-in-unity. His aim in this portrait is to depict a God who is living and therefore consists of multiple constituents which interact with one another in a dialectical process. In other words, God is to be conceived analogously to the living organic beings of the world. The process which is God's life is the means whereby he freely attains the stability of his own being (through a complex process of opposition in subduing the ground in himself). In creating the world which exists in addition to himself God reproduces in it the same ontological structure which he possesses. Therefore the world exists contingently but its essence is necessary (because it is structurally parallel to God himself).[4]

The *Stuttgart Lectures* state in a more precise way the process of self-differentiation which occurs in God. Schelling is now clear that this process is the means whereby God comes to self-consciousness. Here he describes God's self-unfolding as a series of oppositions of the real and ideal poles. The real-ideal contrast is also fundamental for the formation of various levels of complexity in the natural world and human nature, which Schelling describes by the doctrine of "potencies" carried forward from his earlier works on the philosophy of nature. He also presents a rudimentary sketch of a philosophy of the "spirit world."[5] *Ages* picks up all these threads in a complex speculative account of the structure of God.

In *Ages* Schelling presents the most sophisticated version of his portrait of God as a voluntary duality-in-unity. This is the final ontological synthesis of the diverse strands he has been working with since he first became obsessed with understanding God and the world in light of the themes of freedom and the dependence of actual being upon will. The synthesis clearly expresses the move from negative philosophy to positive philosophy. The duality in God is constituted by a pole of necessity and a pole of freedom. The necessity pole corresponds to the ground in God of the essay *Of Human Freedom.*

The explication of the necessity in God is the core of the negative philosophy. The necessity pole consists of three components or powers dialectically related to one another. This ensemble of powers is the non-being which is in God.[6] The ensemble of powers undergoes various transformations as it is converted into the fundamental structures of God's realized being and as it reappears later in reduplicated form as the ground of being for the creation. We will see how it eventually becomes the basis for explaining the natures and relations of the Cabiri in *The Deities of Samothrace.*

In simple outline the structure of the triad is as follows. The first power (pure subjectivity) is the force of contraction or inwardness, a self-centeredness drawing everything else to be consumed within it, a striving to negate all other being. The second power (pure objectivity) is an outgoing, expansive force, a self-giving which relates to, and thereby affirms, all other being. Because the two stand to one another as opposed contraries their mutual compatibility can only be accomplished by a third power (unity) which reconciles them. In the necessity in God these three powers stand dialectically related to one another in an unstable situation. The second tends to nullify the first, the third overcomes the ascendancy of the second, and, because the prevalence of the third is unstable, the perpetual process reverts back to the ascendancy of the first and thus begins again. Schelling refers to this as an "eternal process." The dialectical triad is not so much a portrait of an actual "something" in God, as it is an account of the three principles which Schelling thinks must lie at the foundation of being, any being whatsoever (including God's being). He calls the triad of powers God's "past," that is, the substratum of God's being but not a condition which actually obtains in just this format in God's eternally realized being. However, the three are not abstractions in the sense of "mere ideas"; they are instead very real powers which, if left to themselves, would be non-being (*mē on*) in its raw, unstructured character. However, if they be subordinated to a powerful criterion standing external to them and thus constrained to take up a stable and orderly relation to one another, then they constitute the fundamental structures of being. Because for Schelling the being of God is constituted prior to the being of the world, this triad of powers is more appropriately termed the necessity, ground, or non-being in God. It is what must be overcome or brought under control in order for God to be. The rational dialectic which reflects upon the powers of the necessity in God is the negative philosophy.

The external criterion to which the triad is subordinated is the freedom in God. The pole of freedom is not "a being" but instead is pure will, which is the highest reality. Schelling is a metaphysical voluntarist with respect to God. In God (who is complex) the highest principle is a pure will to which God's own realized being is subordinate. Will of itself doesn't have a content. The content (i.e. the being) which God wills for himself derives from the three powers in the necessity pole. When subordinated to will, the powers are transformed so that they can coexist harmoniously with one another instead of tending to displace one another. At this point in his account Schelling draws heavily upon Neoplatonic conceptions. The subordination and transformation of the powers occurs merely by virtue of the freedom pole's presence to them. It does not have to "act" upon them. In the Neoplatonic system The One does not act causally upon the world, but rather the lower levels of reality spontaneously orient themselves toward it and form an ordered hierarchy of being in response to its sheer presence. In a parallel account Schelling says that the transmuted powers of the ground in God, in the presence of the pole of freedom or pure will, form an ontological hierarchy which is the actual being of God.[7] In this hierarchy the third potency takes the highest position, i.e. it has the greatest ontological proximity to the freedom in God; the first potency takes the lowest. An important factor to keep in mind, especially when we come to the interpretation of the Samothracian cult, is that the third potency is not, like the others, an element with a constitution of its own. Schelling describes it as a principle ordering the relation of the other two, by virtue of the intermediary role which it plays between what is ontologically superior to it, and what is below it. The presence of the freedom pole enables the third potency to mediate between it and the first two potencies, thus establishing the stable hierarchy which is God's being. This process whereby God's actual being is constituted is "eternal." That is, it does not occur in time. God quite simply and freely "is" this way.[8]

It is very important to note that God's self-constitution or "eternal becoming" is also described as his attaining of self-consciousness. When the powers of the necessity pole are transmuted into God's being, this provides for the freedom pole (the "highest" element of God) a concrete realization of itself in an "other" (i.e. a being or essence). In beholding this, its being, freedom is conscious of itself. God as the complex of freedom, necessity (as "past") and realized being, is eternally self-conscious and eternally living. Therefore God really is the eternal paradigm for all the processes of life, consciousness, and self-consciousness which will arise later (through the medium of actual oppositions) in the creation itself.

The same sequence of three potencies is reproduced twice more at lower levels in Schelling's ontology, each time as a hierarchy with the third at the top in the role of organizer of the other two and mediating agent with the next higher level of being. The next reduplication occurs in the realm of the "divine ideas," or the image in God's mind of a possible creation. The possible creation consists of the same three potencies, and thus has an ontological structure paralleling, or replicating, that of God's realized being. The possible creation is likewise eternal, for it does not come to be in God's mind in a temporal process. This ideal world corresponds in function, if not in detailed structure, to the realm of "ideas in the mind of God" according to Christian Platonism and also Aquinas. All three potencies coexist in it harmoniously and eternally.

The final reduplication of the triad of potencies occurs in the creation of the actual world, in which there first appears actual time as a series of sequential, rather than just ontological, relationships. Thus the ontological structure of the world is given by the structure of God himself. Schelling's metaphysical voluntarism structures his doctrine of creation in two important respects. First, God's decision to create is absolutely free. There is no necessity that the possible creation in the divine mind become actual. Creation is contingent with regard to its existence. Second, the creatures themselves have free will. They can allow the disruptive power of non-being to break out in their own beings in a way that it cannot do in God (for in God it is eternally overcome). In the world each of the three potencies tends to predominate in a different sphere. The first is the foundation of physical nature (the "real"), the second of the "spirit world" (the "ideal"), and the third is the link of the first two with the higher reality, which is God.[9] Schelling's two-level account of the potencies in God's eternally actualized being and in the possible world in the divine mind constitutes the first or rationally deductive part of the positive philosophy. The second or empirical part of the positive philosphy begins with the account of the created world, and continues in its fuller form with the history of the divine life in the world, recounted in mythology and revelation.

A perplexing problem throughout Schelling's authorship from 1809 on is whether or to what extent God has a transcendent being. Is his being fully actualized independently of the world, or is it perhaps identifiable with the world-process itself? In *Of Human Freedom* and the *Stuttgart Lectures* the distinction between the two is not clearly drawn. This seems excusable in light of the fact that Schelling has here a new position in the process of formation, and that *Ages* eventually follows with a doctrine which clearly affirms that God has a transcendent, completely actualized being, independent of the world. In *Ages* God's participation in the world occurs as a consequence of the fact that God's being in a sense encloses the world within itself. However, when we press further into the empirical part of the positive philosophy the emphasis falls instead on God's participation in the developing life of the world.[10] His immanence comes to the fore and his transcendence recedes somewhat from our attention as Schelling moves on from the God of speculative ontology to the God known through nature and history. But once God's participation in the world is taken as the principal object of attention, there is the possibility of collapsing the distinction between God's self-realization and his self-revelation. If one supposes that God's presence in and to the world (in Christian terms, the historical appearance of the Son) enhances or adds to God's being, then the world-process itself would be viewed as the vehicle for God's complete self-realization.[11] Schelling resists such a maneuver by continuing to speak of God as transcendent and as coming to the world rather than coming to be through the world. Yet as he ventures into the philosophy of mythology and revelation there is an obvious shift to a treatment of God's self-manifestation in the world which, in terms of the constituents of the divine, proceeds "from the bottom up." This process occurs over time, so the potencies come to be called "periods of God's self-revelation." Accordingly, in *The Deities of Samothrace* the Cabiri sequence commences with the primordial disclosure of the divine in the world and points ahead toward God's future full manifestation.

2. The Symbolism of the Cabiri

The metaphysical interpretation of the Cabiri-natures builds upon a variety of images extracted from the ancient literary sources. Schelling emphasizes those which are similar to, or the same as, the imagery from the writings of Boehme which he allowed to color the abstract ontology of his writings from *Of Human Freedom* to *Ages*.

The first Cabiri deity is Axieros (identified with Demeter-Ceres). Based on Schelling's assessment of Phoenician-Hebrew roots, her name means "hunger" or "poverty." In a derivative sense she is one who is "seeking" or "yearning" for something else, an emptiness seeking a counterpart to receive into itself. Other images which he mentions are: the night, reaching out to receive the light; the consuming fire; the feminine, considered as receptivity (351 - 353).

> Another image of that first nature, whose whole essence is desire and passion, appears in the consuming fire which so to speak is itself nothing, is in essence only a hunger drawing everything into itself. Hence the ancient precept: fire is the most inward, therefore also the oldest; through the subduing of fire everything first began to be a world. (352)
>
> For the burning desire must precede the satisfied desire, and the greatest receptivity, thus consuming hunger, must precede the abundant fullness of fecundity. (353)

Schelling supports his interpretation with many citations from ancient authors.[12] But the strking point in his analysis is the correspondence between the characteristics he chooses to highlight in the body of the text itself, and the salient characteristics of the first potency of being according to *Ages*. In the Samothracian cult Axieros (together with Axiokersa, as we will soon see) is the mythological-religious symbol for the most fundamental of the constitutive powers of being.

Two general metaphysical points mentioned in passing in this section deserve notice. The first point is based on the role of Axieros as the "first being ⟨*Wesen*⟩, commencing all" (352). Here "*Wesen*" means "nature" or "principle," rather than "entity." The deity symbolizes that which is not itself a specific thing, that is, she stands for the first power of *Ages* which is one of the constitutives of being, and thus of all beings. The second point is based on the deities' order of rank.

> [The first is also the lowest.] Everything lowest, beneath which there is nothing further, can only be seeking, a nature which is not insofar as it merely strives to be. (353)

The progression of deities represents an ascent in levels of being and value rather than a descent or decline as in emanation doctrines.

The second deity of the Cabiri is Axiokersa (equivalent to Persephone-Proserpina). Schelling stresses the point that this name (as does the following one) contains the same root as Ceres (Keres), going back to the Hebrew *ḥrš*,*

> . . .a new verification of the otherwise known fact that Proserpina is just Ceres, the daughter just the mother in another form, and that even their names were interchanged, as often their images. (355)

Therefore Axiokersa does not stand for the second power or potency, as we might have anticipated, but rather for the first under another aspect. Axiokersa-Persephone possesses magical powers, a characteristic shared with her mother, Axieros-Ceres, who is said to be

> . . . the moving power through whose ceaseless attraction everything, as if by magic, is brought from the primal indeterminateness to actuality or formation. (355)[13]

Persephone is really the same as that originally formless fire goddess, Hestia (Vesta), but only when she (Hestia) is transposed into form as "the living magic." Whereas the first of the Cabiri can be equated with the first power of *Ages* in its pure, unstructured aspect in the necessity pole in God, the second Cabiri goddess symbolizes that power as transformed into the first potency, which is the foundation of a dimension, or a region, of actual being. Axiokersa is therefore the divine appearance in the corporeal world, i.e. that aspect of God which underlies and permeates the physical universe.[14]

Axiokersos (Hades) is actually Dionysos, who symbolizes the second, or spiritual, level of being.[15] In his *Stuttgart Lectures* Schelling had developed in outline form a "philosophy of the spirit world."[16] In his philosophy of nature summarized therein the corporeal universe is under the predominant influence of the first potency (although corporeal being does consist of all three potencies, as must any instance of actual being). The spirit world partially arises within the corporeal universe, through the higher functions of human nature (philosophy, morality, art). But the spirit world is to be fully actualized only in an afterlife which souls enter upon death. Axiokersos-Dionysos symbolizes the dominion of the second potency, that aspect of the divine which reveals itself in the created world of spiritual being. In the *Stuttgart Lectures* Schelling depicted the spirit world as evolving (ontologically, if not chronologically) from the corporeal world as its foundation. The magical powers of Persephone carry over to Dionysos who, as Schelling believes (although he cannot support it from ancient texts), has a higher form of magic. Ceres-Persephone ignites the living fire of the world. Dionysos

> ... banks it ... moderates it and thereby becomes the first initiator of nature, opening it up into mild life and gentle corporeality. (Note 64)
>
> Axiokersa and Axiokersos together construct the cosmos through a twofold magic, for the later one does not counteract or cancel out the earlier, but rather subdues it. (Note 64)

The spirit world arises out of the corporeal world which serves as its foundation. The presence of the spirit world gives ontological stability to the corporeal world. Beyond both, and in its worldly manifestation arising from them, is the third potency.

The third potency in its mythical-religious manifestation is symbolized by the fourth of the Cabiri series, a male deity variously named Kasmilos, Kadmilos, or Camillus. He is by common consent a servant or attendant figure. In whose service does he stand? The prevailing scholarly opinion (Sainte-Croix, Creuzer) was that he is servant (hence subordinate) to those deities preceding him in the list. Schelling takes strong exception to this view on the plausible grounds that Mnaseas equates Kadmilos with Hermes or Mercury. Hermes is the servant or messenger of Zeus, the high god in Greek mythology. In Schelling's view, Kadmilos is the mediator between the first three Cabiri, who are subordinate to him, and the higher gods. Therefore in a sense he "serves" both those deities above him and those below him, as the effective bond between them (357f.).[17]

In *Ages* the third potency, unlike the other two, is not characterized as the foundation for its own specific sphere of being. Instead, it is that which establishes the harmonious and stable relation between the other two potencies, and thereby integrates them with itself as an ordered hierarchy subordinate to what stands above it (ontologically). The third potency is the mediator which subordinates the necessity pole (including itself) in God to the pole of freedom, and by this subordination constitutes God's realized being. Likewise it is the highest level within the "divine ideas," mediating between them and God's being proper. In addition, the third potency reappears in Schelling's system as the mediator between the actual creation (corporeal and spiritual) and God. In carrying through his systematic interpretation, how natural then for Schelling to impress this ontologically mediating role upon (or find it in) the figure of Kadmilos.

As mediator, Kadmilos is the harbinger of that which is higher than himself, "the herald of the coming god" (358). His serving role is comparable to that of the Old Testament "angel of the presence," the one who goes before Yahweh.[18] The god whom Kadmilos serves is a future god, whose coming he awaits and proclaims.

> Thus the names positively point to a future god to which Kadmilos or Hermes himself, and so necessarily also the gods preceding him, relate only as subordinated. . . . Far from following in descending order, the gods succeed one another in ascending order. (358)

The four known Cabiri symbolize a hierarchy of powers, constituted "from the bottom up." They are a divine revelation in the world of the three potencies of Schelling's ontology, hence the disclosure in myth of three fundamental constituents of his God. At this point Schelling digresses to attack the emanation theory in general, and its application to the religion of Samothrace in particular.

Schelling praises Creuzer for showing definitively that Ceres is the first of the Cabiri-natures. But Creuzer erred grievously in depicting Ceres as the highest deity, and thus followed the mistaken lead of Zoëga in imposing an emanationist interpretation upon the Samothracian pantheon (note 74). Schelling's case for an ascending sequence is based both on the role of Kadmilos, which is inconsistent with an emanationist interpretation, and on his concern to read the Samothracian mythology as an exemplification of his own ontology. But he also presents another argument of a general sort. The idea of the unity of God is "humanly necessary and indelible" (358f.). However, the emanation theory cannot explain adequately why the multiple deities of polytheism present themselves to the believer as such distinctive and worthy objects of human worship. Emanations from a highest One are inherently inferior to it, and should be recognized as such and bypassed by the devotion of the wise. Yet the initiates into the secret doctrines worshipped all of the Cabiri "as links of a chain ascending from the depths to the heights." As mediators announcing and preparing for the coming of the highest god, they properly share in his glory.

> This fact alone explains how the honor rendered to the multiple gods strikes roots so deep and almost ineradicable, how it can maintain itself for so long. Therefore the notion of emanation seems suited neither for the interpretation of ancient mythology in general, nor for the interpretation of Samothracian mythology in particular. Here it founders on the correctly understood concept of Kadmilos. (359)

Schelling also rejects Warburton's hypothesis that ancient mystery cults such as that of Samothrace secretly taught monotheism, while preserving a semblance of polytheism in the public cult. To him this hypothesis represents a blatant imposition of Enlightenment theology (a "Mohammedan," unbiblical monotheism) upon antiquity, without the slightest historical warrant for doing so (316f.).

In fact Schelling's rejection of the hypothesis of an original or primordial monotheism, and his rejection of an emanationist reading of the Samothracian pantheon, are all of a piece. For him the self-disclosure of God in the world must be "progressive," beginning with the first potency and only gradually moving toward the fullness of the divine presence to the creation. That is why the movement of history is from mythology to revelation, and why the higher Cabiri natures are only intimated in the Samothracian mythology, for they are aspects of the "coming god," whose full appearance in the world awaits the time of revelation. (Cf. section three which follows).

The first four Cabiri taken together are the divine analogy in the world to what in God is the necessity pole as subordinated to the pole of freedom.

> First of all it is clear that those initial deities are the very same powers through whose action and rule the whole world chiefly was constituted; thus it is clear that they are worldly, cosmic deities. Collectively they are called Hephaestos . . . (360)

The powers of the necessity in God undergird what God "eternally becomes" in his actual being. Similarly, the first four Cabiri are "the innerworldly seat of the gods," a living progression of powers in the universe which are

> . . . only the epiphany, preparing the revelation of the higher gods. . . they are not so much divine as they are god-producing, theurgic natures, and the whole chain presents itself more and more as theurgic. . . so the god to whom they are the leader and ladder, whom Kadmilos directly serves, is the *transcendent* god, the god who rules them and thus is lord of the world, the demiurge or, in the highest sense, Zeus. (360f.)[19]

This Zeus, equated with the Old Testament "El" (360), will be the fullest development of divine personality in the world, transfiguring in itself those lower theurgic natures (which are not fully personal themselves, but only constituents of the divine personality) (359).

As a group the Cabiri were called "the great" and "the mighty." That they were sometimes depicted as dwarfs is only an apparent anomaly, for the dwarf or pygmy form is frequently associated with beings of great magical powers.[20] Together they stand in inseparable union.

> Yet not singly, but only in their insoluble sequence and chain do they practice the magic by which the transcendent is drawn into reality. . . only in concert are the Cabiri the great salvation-bringing gods, and they are honored not singly, but only in common. (366)

This complex interdependence of these deities receives from Schelling yet a further metaphysical and numerical explication, with which I conclude the philosophical analysis of the inner meaning of the Samothracian cult.

Schelling can harmonize his interpretation with the position attributed to Varro (in Creuzer) that the oldest version of the Cabiri doctrine spoke of two deities. That is because the two are "principles of the divine" *(principes Dei)*, rather than individual personalities exclusive of others.

> For all philosophy is led to such a duality lying at the basis of all, without thereby maintaining that there are only two *beings* *(Wesen)*. (Note 112)

The two are of course the first and second potencies, symbolized as Ceres-Persephone and Dionysos. The opposition of the two requires a third to unite them, hence even Varro's dualism becomes a triadic schema. (Recall once again that for Schelling the third potency is not actually a separate nature, but rather that which unites the other two and binds them to what is "higher.") Because the potencies of being are not exhausted in whatever severally exemplifies or symbolizes them, they can recur at various levels within an extended hierarchy. In addition, the character of one potency can be present as a recessive influence in that which is under the dominant influence of a different potency. This possibility accounts for the fact that a deity can share secondarily in a quality possessed by another in a primary sense (e. g. Dionysos can be a demiurge, too, although Zeus is *the* demiurge.) It also explains how the universe and the deities can be structured in triadic arrangements, some of which are inclusive of others.

> . . . a nature ⟨*Wesen*⟩ or principle which stands higher than another and to that extent is its contrast (prevailing over it), nevertheless can with that one belong to one class over against a still higher (principle). . . . Zeus is also again Dionysos. . . . That is, Zeus is again related to the first three potencies, as the second is related to the first. (Note 80)

There are seven Cabiri, or perhaps eight. Schelling supplies us with the names and his interpretations of the first four, plus reference to the transcendent god who is to come, Zeus who is the seventh. History doesn't provide us with the names of numbers five and six. Neither does Schelling, although in filling in the details of his system one would expect them to be "coming deities," too, transmuted versions of the first two potencies taken up as constituents in the actualized Zeus. But Zeus is also number eight.

> Hereby Jupiter must be conceived in a double relation: once, insofar as he himself is one of the seven; then insofar as he is Zeus the beginning, Zeus the middle, and Zeus the end, as the Orphics say. (Note 117)

The eighth contains the other seven within itself, just as in the panentheism of the *Stuttgart Lectures* and *Ages* God's eternal being is the paradigm for real time, and embraces within itself the whole of creation with its three ages of past, present, and future. In one sense the true God reveals himself successively in the moments of time and history; in another sense he is the unity of the process, for it unfolds within himself.

3. Toward the Philosophy of Mythology and Revelation

The Deities of Samothrace is the beginning of a project which Schelling perhaps originally thought could be handled within the compass of *Ages* itself.[21] But certainly by October of 1815 he had recognized something of the effort and scope required by the new project, for in his postscript to *The Deities of Samothrace* he referred the reader both backward to *Ages* and forward to the investigations yet to come.

> Not in itself but only in the intention of the author a supplement to another work, it is at once a beginning and a transition to some others the intention of which is to bring the actual primordial system of humanity to light from long eclipse, according to scientific development and where possible in an historical manner. (423)

Although the foundation was laid by 1815, it wasn't until many years later that Schelling set down in systematic form and in detail his promised philosophy of mythology and revelation.[22] This final section offers a brief summary of themes from Schelling's philosophy of mythology and also situates within this structure *The Deities of Samothrace,* as an example of the mystery religions which constitute the point of transition to the philosophy of revelation.

In the initial presentation of the positive philosophy in *Ages* there are two crucial junctures at which further expression of the potencies depends upon an act of will. The first occurs when the freedom in God wills to control the powers in the necessity pole and to convert them into the ordered potencies of God's actualized being. The second occurs when God freely wills to create a world in addition to himself, a world which embodies the same three potencies but now as external to him. Therefore to philosophize about God's actual being or about the world's being is to begin not with a purely rational deduction, but instead with a "fact." The positive philosophy is "positive" precisely because its point of departure is a "given." The being which the positive philosophy interprets *is* only because it is willed to be and not because of any rational necessity that it be.

Schelling's subsequent philosophy of religion is an exposition of God's self-disclosure in nature and history. Revelation is grounded in God's will expressed in his free act. The content of the self-disclosure is not derivable from reason itself. It can only come to us from experience, that is, from the facts of the natural world and the historical process as God acts in them. It is true that the speculative doctrine of God found in *Ages* gives clues as to what to expect, for Schelling carried forward not only into *The Deities of Samothrace* but also into all of his subsequent philosophy of religion the doctrine of potencies from the negative and positive philosophy as presented in *Ages.*[23] Yet it is only from study of the actual structures of nature and the events of history that the full knowledge of God can be obtained. The course of mythology and revelation takes its shape from two "facts" which do not, strictly speaking, occur out of necessity (despite appearances to the contrary in some of Schelling's statements) but instead derive from the free exercise of will. These facts are unknowable from an exclusively speculative consideration of God. They are the fall of humanity and God's decision to involve himself in the world in such a way as to bring his fallen creation back to himself.

The fall cannot be demonstrated a priori from rational principles, nor can it be treated as a specific adventure which befell an historical individual. On this issue Schelling is at home neither with speculative idealism nor with biblical orthodoxy. Fallenness is simply a fact of the world as centered in humanity, a fact for which God is not responsible. Although the fall is not knowable as a particular event, its consequences are experienced in the world.[24] Humanity's fall casts the created potencies out of their harmonious co-existence and into mutual opposition, thus establishing a whole series of evil consequences. Humanity is sinful, for it freely elevates the power of subjectivity or negativity into the position of supremacy. Each person is a self-centered individual, subject to the fate of all willfully estranged individuals, which is eventual death. A concomitant result is the fallenness of the cosmos itself. All its members are subjected to existence in spatial and temporal separation from one another. These developments are symptomatic of the fundamental fact that the fall unleashes the power which underlies the first potency in all its forms in God and creation, the destructiveness of unrestrained self-centeredness or negativity. To conquer this independent assertion of the power of negativity God freely wills to act in the world to reconcile the creatures to one another and to himself. The historical records of mythology and of the revealed religions portray the dynamics of the divine action and thereby disclose the actual nature of God.

God acts through the agency of the second potency in the world to overcome the independent and unruly manifestation of the first potency. The victory restores the first to its proper subordinate relation to the second. The eventual perfecting of this harmony will be the full expression of the third potency, the completed future reconciliation of the world internally with itself and also with God. The history of human religion is the locus of this divine activity of revelation and reconciliation. The religious consciousness of humanity throughout history is an evolving awareness of the successive stages of the struggle in which the second potency develops from its initial manifestations in the creation to its full arrival in power. The mythology of ancient religions contains human consciousness of the preliminary stages of the struggle. The pinnacle of revealed religion (which for Schelling is Christianity) discloses the full appearance and decisive victory of the second potency. In trinitarian terms, the second potency is the Son and the final rule of the third potency will be the age of the Spirit. The Greek mystery religion finds its place in the schema as the culmination of the ancient mythological process and the forerunner of revelation proper. Therefore the mysteries of Samothrace exemplify that type of religious expression which sums up the import of preceding mythological intuitions and foreshadows the full disclosure of the divine.

The mythological process commences when the second potency begins to liberate human consciousness from its bondage to the first potency. The deities of mythological consciousness stand in close connection with natural forces.[25] However they do not simply spring from a human propensity to deify natural objects. They display the divine in and through the medium of natural processes, but without being reducible merely to nature itself. Because nature and mythology lie in that realm over which the first potency prevails, in them

God is hidden as well as revealed. There is a genuine disclosure of God in the mythological process because the three potencies in their divine expression are the final content toward which it leads and because as it advances to its higher levels the potencies show themselves more clearly through the natural symbols.[26] There is hiddenness because the specific natural deities of mythology which represent or symbolize the potencies do so, especially at the lower stages, in a sometimes random or irrational way.

The initial epochs of mythological consciousness can be passed over quickly because the presence and influence of the second potency is relatively ineffectual in them.[27] The first Schelling calls "Uranos," for in this epoch religious attention turns toward the heavens and the stars and planets which represent the divine. The second epoch is "Urania," for in it the divine is depicted as female, as the first potency restored to the status of potentiality from which the second potency could bring forth distinctive forms.

The third epoch of mythological consciousness is the most complex and important one, for it carries the symbolism toward completion. Its preliminary levels, the religions of Canaan-Phoenicia and of Phrygia, make way for the great mythological systems of Egypt, India, and Greece. In the latter systems we see an ambitious but not ultimately successful attempt to break free from the dominion of the first potency and to give adequate representation to the divine as spirit, that is, as the second potency ruling over the first. Egyptian religion valiantly strives to establish certain spiritual or intelligible deities such as Amon, but it fails fully to overcome the first potency because its chief mythology remains focused on animal deities. Indian religion presses to the opposite extreme, relegating the first potency to the background but at the price of attaining merely an abstract and world-denying expression of the second. It is the mythology of the Greeks that finally intimates that true spirituality which reconciles the potencies under the predominance of the third, Hades and Poseidon living under the rule of Zeus.

Nevertheless Greek mythology cannot provide an adequate portrait of the divine because it attains a merely ideal spirituality, one which is unable to grasp the fact that the fallenness of the world is overcome by an act of will on God's part, namely his decision to act in the world to accomplish the reconciliation. The rational development of Greek mythology leads it away from the sphere of religion. Greek mythology becomes the womb of philosophy; the gods of the myths are replaced by the Ideas of the philosophers. Instead the mystery cults of the Greeks are the true heirs to the religious dynamic of the mythological process, for they point in the direction of the coming revelation. In their exoteric dimension they provide the most adequate symbolism for the "natural" manifestations of the divine toward which the entire mythological process proceeds. In their esoteric teachings they point beyond the natural sphere and toward the full coming in power of the second potency. The initiates anticipate the imminent arrival of the future God, when the divine *personality* itself will enter the historical process.[28]

Schelling analyzes the mystery religions in detail in the first or preliminary part of his philosophy of revelation. Here he takes into account not just the Samothracian cult, but the overall pattern of the ancient mysteries. As in the case of the first four Samothracian deities, so with the exoteric teaching of the mysteries in general, there is a sequence of deities beginning with Demeter which symbolizes the divine through the medium of natural forces. The esoteric doctrine is organized around three forms of Dionysos, associated respectively with past, present, and future, and standing for the three potencies of being. The entire series of deities points finally to the coming of the third and future Dionysos in whom they find their fulfillment. The specific symbolism interpreted by Schelling varies from the earlier to the later work. But the basic import of the mysteries is already laid out in 1815 in *The Deities of Samothrace*. The figures of Axieros, Axiokersa, Axiokersos, and Kadmilos fully symbolize the divine as manifested through natural forces and processes. The esoteric doctrines of Samothrace, involving deities whose names have not come down to us, foreshadow the coming revelation in which God himself will be personally present to his world,

> the *transcendent* god, the god who rules them and thus is lord of the world, the demiurge or, in the highest sense, Zeus. (360f.)

This is the point of transition to revelation proper.

In this monograph I have shown the importance of *The Deities of Samothrace* as the stepping-stone from the abstract ontology of *Ages* to the complexity of the positive philosophy of religion. Schelling himself foresaw the significance of this investigation and in his postscript stressed this very point.

> Not by chance do the particulars of the Samothracian system precede the more general inquiry; it was intentional to lay this at the foundation; for the Cabiri doctrine is as a key to all the rest. . . .(423)

In this exploratory treatise Schelling exhibited what later would prove to be for him the critical link between mythology and revelation, because in the Samothracian cult

> . . . . the basic idea remains indestructible, the whole of the original doctrine unmistakable, a belief rescued from remote primitive times which, of all paganism, is purest and closest to the truth. (369)

Notes to Part Three

[1] In the following exposition of Schelling's conception of God in the works prior to *The Deities of Samothrace*, I make no attempt to document the many points presented in summary fashion. That has been done elsewhere, in my book mentioned in the bibliography. In any case these points as made here in a general fashion are not subjects of scholarly controversy.

²*Philosophie und Religion* (1804), 6, 11-70 (4, 1-60).

³Schelling employs the Platonic tradition's distinction between *mē on,* and *ouk on.* Non-being as *ouk on* is "nothing at all," the complete absence of anything. Non-being as *mē on* is potentiality, that which could be (something) but is not. For Plotinus *mē on* is matter, the recalcitrant substratum upon which the forms are impressed to produce actual beings. However, Schelling makes two important variations. He preserves Plotinus' framework but redescribes *mē on* as raw power without structure, the ground of being which left to itself is uncontrolled destructiveness but which, subjected to suitable restraints, becomes actual beings. Schelling also (without admitting that he is doing it) alters the traditional theological doctrine of "creation out of nothing" by saying it refers to *mē on,* not *ouk on.* The upshot is that he can say God has a pole of non-being (*mē on*) in himself which is the ground of his own being and, by extension, also the ground of the being of the creation as well.

⁴*Of Human Freedom* also deals with the themes of theodicy and of human free will. In it Schelling does not adequately distinguish God's process of self-actualization from his activity of creating the world. Therefore he gives the false impression (remedied in the following works) that God is compelled by some ontological necessity to create, in order to carry out his own self-actualization.

⁵Real and ideal poles are two aspects of all being. Both are present in all actual beings, but in each instance one pole predominates and the other pole is latent or subordinate. In Schelling's philosophy of nature (which has its counterpart in the analysis of God's nature), a potency is a level of being characterized by a particular relation of real and ideal aspects. The first potency encompasses corporeal being or nature, for in it the real emerges first and prevails over the ideal. The second potency embraces the first but goes beyond it to constitute the spirit world (including human nature as subjective), for in it the ideal rules. The third potency surpasses and is the reconciliation of the first two (which tend to conflict among themselves). Its paradigms are the eternal harmony of God's realized being, and the reconciliation of all of nature and spirit with one another and with God at the end of time.

⁶The triad of powers is a transmuted version of the first three of the seven "qualities" which constitute God, according to Jacob Boehme's thought. Schelling appropriated this schema from Boehme and integrated the borrowed material with elements from the doctrine of potencies in his own earlier philosophy of nature.

⁷ Further on in *Ages* Schelling introduces a terminological distinction between "power" and "potency." Powers are simple forces which are mutually exclusive. They coexist in the necessary pole in the sense that they continually replace one another. A potency is complex. The first potency contains both the first and second powers, with the first predominant. In the second potency, the second power predominates over the first. The third potency is a special case, as will be pointed out below. If the powers are subdued to form the potencies (in the first instance, God's being), the potencies coexist as separated or "spread out" into an ontological hierarchy. The hierarchy of potencies is stable, whereas the ensemble of dialectically related powers is not. From this point on Schelling speaks of potencies rather than powers.

⁸God is temporally prior to the world. But with regard to God's own constitution all references to certain elements or stages as being "before" or "prior to" others should be understood as indicative of ontological, not temporal, priority. There is no sequential time in God. The process of his self-constitution is eternal, i.e. all elements of it co-exist "simultaneously." Nevertheless, the ontological relations obtaining eternally within God are the paradigms of temporal relations. If a replica of these eternal ontological relations would develop sequentially there would be actual time. This is just what happens subsequently in the creation which God makes. So for Schelling there is a special sense in which it can be said that there is (an "eternal") time in God. At this point he is in fundamental agreement with the Platonic definition of time as "the moving image of eternity" (*Timaeus* 37Df.).

⁹The full account of this threefold structure of the world occurs in the *Stuttgart Lectures,* not in *Ages.* It correlates closely with the doctrine of potencies present in Schelling's earlier philosophy of nature.

[10]*Ages* also makes an abortive beginning of the empirical part of the positive philosophy but breaks off before the attempt gets very far. My statement about the shift in emphasis regarding the God-World relation refers to the works after *Ages*.

[11]Therefore is the world in some sense necessary for God after all, in order that his own being can be fully actualized? This is a major problem that confronts one in interpreting the philosophy of mythology and revelation.

[12] Ancient sources cited to connect these images with Demeter-Ceres include: Pausanias, *Arcad.* 8.9 — fire; various hymns to Ceres — yearning desire; Ovid, *Meta.* 8.785 — hunger; a myth of the world-egg and the origin of the gods — night. Schelling associates the longing of Demeter with the status of the shades in the underworld, according to both Athenian and Hebrew sources. He also invokes his Phoenician sources.

[13] According to Liddell and Scott, *ta thea* in the dual always refers specifically to this pair, Ceres-Persephone. (Cf. Schelling's note 49 on the *diōnumoi theai.*) Persephone is called "*Maja*," and is a sorceress or conjurer (355). Schelling's search for the original meaning of "*magia*" is inconclusive (note 53, p. 385, not translated here).

[14]In his note 80 Schelling also gives a Pythagorean explanation of the reason why Ceres by herself is not the first potency.

[15]Despite Mnaseas' declaration that Axiokersos is Hades, Schelling defends his identification with a twofold argument. First, a text attributed to Heraclitus says that Hades and Dionysos are one and the same (note 58). Second, Dionysos himself is said to be lord of the spirits of the dead (note 59). Thus Axiokersos-Dionysos is functionally equivalent to the Egyptian Osiris (and to the German Othin).

[16]Cf. 7, 478-82. (4, 370-74).

[17]In interpreting a quotation from Varro which refers to Kadmilos as "servant of the great gods," Schelling points out that the Cabiri were collectively called "the great," and that there were altogether seven (or eight) of them, although not all their names are known (357).

[18]Cf. Schelling's notes 71 and 72. He specifically calls the reader's attention to *Ages,* 8, 272-74 (4, 648-50), where he previously mentioned this biblical figure, the "angel of the presence." In note 84 he speculates that the biblical priest Melchizedek (Gen. 14:18) may have been the first one to whom was revealed the system of the first four Cabiri.

[19]This favorite image of a chain extending upward, linking lower with higher, first with last, is also employed in *Ages,* 8, 290 (4, 666).

[20]Recall that Schelling links the root of the word "theurgy" with the German word for "dwarf"(*Zwerg*) (365).

[21]The earlier drafts and fragments of *Ages* presented in Schröter's *Nachlassband* contain some materials on topics which Schelling cut from the 1815 version but subsequently took up again in the later works.

[22]These massive texts, which were first published in 1856-1861 from Schelling's own manuscripts, occupy more than 2000 pages in the two editions of the collected works. All of these manuscripts date from 1841-1852.

[23]Paul Tillich emphasized this point in his doctoral dissertation, *The Construction of the History of Religion in Schelling's Positive Philosophy: Its Presuppositions and Principles,* translated by Victor Nuovo (Lewisburg, Pa.: Bucknell University Press, 1974).

> The task of the present work is to present the construction of the history of religion as the focal point of Schelling's positive philosophy. This, however, is only possible in the light of the epistemological and metaphysical principles of the whole system. Without the doctrine of the potencies one cannot even set foot in the positive philosophy. (p. 41)

Tillich presents a valuable, although quite condensed and abstract, survey of the contents of the philosophy of mythology and revelation.

[24]Schelling's doctrine of the fall is more complex and philosophically sophisticated than these simplified statements can indicate. However, to pursue it in detail would lead into conceptual difficulties somewhat far afield from the theme under consideration here.

²⁵Mythology can arise only when there is a polytheism in which diverse gods compete with and succeed one another. "Before" mythology there would be a different kind of polytheism in which the divine consists of multiple but mutually compatible expressions of itself. This could be regarded as a kind of monotheism which is logically presupposed as that "prior" condition the breakup of which sets in motion the mythological process. But such a condition was not actually a stage in human history. Therefore this conception is not a repudiation by Schelling of his earlier critique in *The Deities of Samothrace* of the "original monotheism" hypothesis.

²⁶It must be remembered that each potency also contains the others within itself under the dominance of its own distinctive characteristic. Therefore although the second potency is the agent of God's action and self-disclosure to overcome the world's fallenness, the content of the self-revelation is the three potencies in their mutually harmonious relation, as they are in God. Mythology attempts to express this harmony, but only the subsequent revelation succeeds in doing so.

²⁷Schelling's account of mythology is extended and complex. These brief remarks follow the general outlines of Tillich's digest of the material in *The Construction of the History of Religion*. . . .

²⁸*The* religion of revelation is Christianity, for the coming of the divine Son into the world is the full manifestation of the second potency. Judaism and Islam also fall under the rubric of revelation although they are inferior to Christianity in a variety of ways. Schelling discusses the religion of China and Persia, and also Buddhism, as deviants from the mythological process which should not be classified with the religions of revelation.

BIBLIOGRAPHY

The scholarly literature on Schelling is vast and grows at an increasing pace. Schneeberger's bibliography contains over 1000 items up through 1953, and several hundred more articles and books have been published since then. Unfortunately rather little secondary literature is available in English and only a small part of that is actually worth reading. Therefore even the very brief bibliography which follows cannot be limited to materials in the English language. It consists of those works cited in this monograph, plus a few others which are of special use to one who wishes to get his general bearings in Schelling or Samothracian studies or who wishes to dig more deeply into some of the specific topics discussed in the philosophical interpretation presented above. The entries are grouped topically rather than alphabetically.

Lewis, Naphtali, editor and translator. *Samothrace: The Ancient Literary Sources.* New York: Pantheon Books, 1958. This is volume 1 of the Bollingen Series, No. LX, *Samothrace: Excavations Conducted by the Institute of Fine Arts of New York University,* edited by Karl Lehmann. It is a complete collection of ancient texts bearing on Samothrace and its cult.

Lehmann, Karl. *Samothrace: A Guide to the Excavations and the Museum.* New York: New York University Press, 1955. A brief overview of the Samothracian excavations and what has been learned from them.

Feldman, Burton and Robert D. Richardson. *The Rise of Modern Mythology 1680-1860.* Bloomington, Ind.: Indiana University Press, 1972. Contains a wide range of selections from modern interpreters of mythology including some who influenced Schelling, and also a few passages in English translation from Schelling's philosophy of mythology.

Schneeberger, Guido. *Friedrich Wilhelm Joseph von Schelling: Eine Bibliographie.* Bern: Francke Verlag, 1954. A reasonably complete bibliography of published items by or about Schelling up through 1953.

Schelling, K. F. A., editor. *Friedrich Wilhelm Joseph von Schellings sämmtliche Werke,* 14 vols. in two divisions. Stuttgart and Augsburg: J. G. Cotta'scher Verlag, 1856-1861. Edited and arranged by Schelling's son, this is the edition according to which citations of Schelling texts are customarily given.

Schröter, Manfred, editor. *Schellings Werke, Nach der Original Ausgabe in neuer Anordnung,* 6 vols. and 6 supplementary vols. Munich: C. H. Beck and R. Oldenbourg, 1927-1959. Supplemented by a *"Nachlassband," Die Weltalter: Fragmente, In den Urfassungen von 1811 und 1813.* Edited by Manfred Schröter. Munich: C. H. Beck'sche Verlagsbuchhandlung, 1946. Schröter's edition contains everything in the 1857-1861 edition, but in rearranged order. The supplementary volume is indispensable for serious students of *Ages* and its relation to the later positive philosophy.

Plitt, G. L., editor. *Aus Schellings Leben: In Briefen,* 3 vols. Leipzig: S. Hirzel, 1869-1870. Long the only collection of Schelling's correspondence, and still indispensable for studying his later career.

Fuhrmans, Horst, editor. *F. W. J. Schelling: Briefe und Dokumente, Vol. I: 1775-1809.* Bonn: H. Bouvier und Co., 1962; *Vol. II: 1775-1803, Zusatzband.* Bonn: Bouvier Verlag Herbert Grundmann, 1973; *Vol. III: 1803-1809, Zusatzband.* Bonn: Bouvier Verlag Herbert Grundmann, 1975. Fuhrmans' collection of correspondence by and to Schelling, now up to 3 volumes, supersedes those parts of Plitt with which it overlaps chronologically.

Tilliette, Xavier. *Schelling, une philosophie en devenir. I: Le système vivant, 1794-1821. II. La dernière philosophie, 1821-1854.* Paris: J. Vrin, 1970. This magisterial work is overwhelming in its scope and erudition. It is now the definitive account of Schelling's overall career.

Gutmann, James, translator. *Schelling: Of Human Freedom.* Chicago: Open Court, 1936.

Bolman, Frederick de Wolfe, Jr., translator. *Schelling: The Ages of the World.* New York: Columbia University Press, 1942.

Brown, Robert F. *The Philosophy of the Later Schelling: Boehme's Influence on the Works of 1809-1815.* Lewisburg, Pa.: Bucknell University Press, 1976.

Fuhrmans, Horst. *Schellings Philosophie der Weltalter: Schellings Philosophie in den Jahren 1806-1821. Zum Problem des Schellingschen Theismus.* Düsseldorf: L. Schwann, 1954.

Tillich, Paul. *The Construction of the History of Religion in Schelling's Positive Philosophy: Its Presuppositions and Principles.* Translated by Victor Nuovo. Lewisburg, Pa.: Bucknell University Press, 1974. Also by Tillich: *Mysticism and Guilt-Consciousness in Schelling's Philosophical Development.* Translated by Victor Nuovo. Lewisburg, Pa.: Bucknell University Press, 1974. These two dissertations by Tillich did much to awaken interest in Schelling's later philosophy. Because they are generally reliable (if somewhat abstract) presentations of Schelling's own thought, their recent appearance in English translation is of great value to Schelling scholarship as well as to Tillich scholarship.

Fackenheim, Emil L. "Schelling's Conception of Positive Philosophy." *Review of Metaphysics,* VII, (1954), 563-82.